The **5 Step Plan** | to Revita━━━ ━ove
Life━━━ ━━━ ━k,
Bre━━━ ━rce

Dating Again

with Courage & Confidence

Fran Greene, L.C.S.W.

Author of *The Flirting Bible*

FAIR WINDS

Quarto is the authority on a wide range of topics.

Quarto educates, entertains and enriches the lives of our readers—enthusiasts and lovers of hands-on living.

www.QuartoKnows.com

© 2017 Quarto Publishing Group USA Inc.
Text © 2017 Fran Greene

First Published in 2017 by Fair Winds Press, an imprint of The Quarto Group,
100 Cummings Center, Suite 265-D, Beverly, MA 01915, USA.
T (978) 282-9590 F (978) 283-2742 QuartoKnows.com

Fair Winds Press titles are also available at discount for retail, wholesale, promotional, and bulk purchase. For details, contact the Special Sales Manager by email at specialsales@quarto.com or by mail at The Quarto Group, Attn: Special Sales Manager, 401 Second Avenue North, Suite 310, Minneapolis, MN 55401, USA.

21 20 19 18 17   1 2 3 4 5

ISBN: 978-1-59233-760-6

Digital edition published in 2017
eISBN: 978-1-63159-417-5

Library of Congress Cataloging-in-Publication Data

Greene, Fran, author.
Dating again with courage and confidence : the five-step plan to revitalize your love life after heartbreak, breakup, or divorce / Fran Greene.
ISBN 9781592337606 (paperback)
Subjects: LCSH: Dating (Social customs) | Divorced people. | Self-confidence.
LCC HQ801 .G6837 2017 | DDC 306.73--dc23
LCCN 2016056544

Design and Illustration: Mattie Wells

Printed in China

The 5 Step Plan

Contents

Introduction

After a breakup, your grief can be crippling. Whether you were married, in a long-term relationship, or in a short-lived but intense one, the loss you experience is real. But a broken heart is temporary. When it heals, you can be even stronger than before–you can love even more deeply and fully than you could have imagined.

That's where this book comes in. In it, I offer a systematic, prescriptive approach to help you get over your breakup and move on toward joy and fulfillment. Think of me as your Breakup Doctor: I'm here to care for you, but I can't do it alone; you need to be involved each step of the way. This book is a participatory process. Your investment is crucial: You'll need to take action and ownership of your healing so you can move through the pain of your breakup and into the life you were meant to lead.

As a relationship expert and professional dating coach, I have interviewed many women who have recovered from breakups or divorces–including some who have experienced multiple breakups. While researching this book, I asked them, "What helped you the most while going through your breakup? What helped bandage your heart when you couldn't stop the bleeding? What did you need to do to gain confidence and get back into the dating world? Which dating tips helped you the most?" And the advice I offer here is based on their remarkable recovery stories–plus my own personal and professional experience. In case you're

wondering if I've ever had my heart broken, the answer is a resounding yes. I've had two major heartbreaks, and lots of mini ones. Here's what it felt like for me:

I finally met a wonderful guy whom I was completely sure I would marry and live happily ever after with. We dated for two years. We had everything in common; we lived together; and it felt like a perfect fit. And then one day he said he wasn't sure of his feelings. I dismissed this; facing it was too scary. Everything returned to normal for a while, and I was 100 percent sure that marriage was on the horizon. Everything was perfect again–or so I thought. Several months later, he told me it was over. I remember hearing the words "It's over," and then I went numb. I heard nothing except my own inner voice, which was screaming at the top of its lungs. "This can't be happening," it shrieked. "My life is over. I'll never meet anyone, I'll never love anyone else, nor will anyone ever love me." I felt paralyzed and cried uncontrollably. It was almost an out of body experience.

But what I learned from heartbreaks like this one was that I needed to be resilient and believe I would find the love of my life—but I couldn't leave it up to chance. I had to take control of my social life and do anything and everything that would bring me closer to finding the love and happiness I knew I deserved. I had to be my biggest cheerleader. And I was. I tried just about everything in my search for the "perfect partner," because I knew that anything really important in life takes effort and work, and I was determined to persevere!

It worked. Lucky me: I met the love of my life, the man who is my amazing husband. He continues to make my life complete, and I couldn't be happier. I love him with all my heart and soul. And my dream is for you, too, to find the love you want and deserve. I'm so glad you've let me into your life to help you do that.

To that end, my job is to get you to move dating to the top of your to-do list, even if you don't want to. Why? Because the longer you put off dating, the more difficult it becomes. Procrastination does have a benefit—you can avoid taking the risk of dating again—but the downside is that your fears will be intensified the longer you wait.

So let's get going! Here's what you can expect in the coming pages. This book is divided into five steps. Each step features exercises or assignments designed to inspire you and to build your confidence so dating will become your new favorite hobby.

Step 1: DECLUTTER

Adjust to Life after a Breakup

Breakups turn your life upside down and inside out, so I've created a Breakup Survival Kit to help you get through the first days and weeks post-breakup. It's chock-full of useful, down-to-earth ways to help you cope with the devastation of your heartbreak. Once you're ready, I'll explain the five stages of grief that characterize the end of every relationship, so you won't feel scared or overwhelmed by them. Then, I'll give you clear-cut directions on how to disconnect from your ex and a menu of options for expressing your thoughts and feelings—which can help kick-start your recovery. I'll encourage you to seek help when you need it—from friends, support groups, and therapists who can all help you make sense of the end of your relationship. I'll walk you through ways to nourish and nurture yourself; show you why decluttering, both literally and metaphorically, is essential to opening your heart and mind post-breakup. I'll be totally honest with you about the risks (and rewards) of rebound relationships. Ultimately, Step 1 will show you that your broken heart will not last forever. You will recover.

Step 2: FIND JOY
Advice for Diving into the Dating Pool with Confidence and Optimism

In this step, you'll celebrate that your heart has healed and your tears are now part of your past. And I'll show you how to overcome your dating fears so you can jump back in and start dating again—this time, with the mindset, "It's Just a Date." (These four words will become your new mantra!) You'll learn how to tell when you're ready to start dating; how to choose a dating coach who will support you and cheer you on through your dating adventures; and you'll find out exactly which "dating rules" you need to break if you want to find lasting love. I have plenty of suggestions for what to do when you're actually on a date, too, so your encounters will be fruitful and fun. In Step 2, your whole attitude toward dating will be transformed, and you'll look forward to it with confidence and joy.

Step 3: FLAUNT IT
Become a Fabulous Flirt

Ever notice how some people are natural flirts? You can be one, too, and Step 3 shows you exactly how. With a little practice, you'll effortlessly create a sense of magic when you meet a stranger—yes, even if you usually shy away from approaching people. You'll learn how to use body language to become more approachable and attractive, exude confidence, and get noticed. And as for what to say to the adorable guy or gal of your dreams? I'll show you how to craft playful, light-hearted opening lines that encourage conversation. By the end of Step 3, you'll be on a 24/7 flirt alert and see opportunities for meeting people just about everywhere.

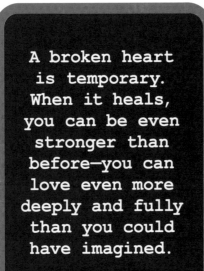

A broken heart is temporary. When it heals, you can be even stronger than before—you can love even more deeply and fully than you could have imagined.

Step 4: MASTER IT

Unlock the Secrets of Online Dating

Step 4 shows you how to maximize your success with online dating, which is how millions of people around the world meet their husbands, wives, and partners. Dating sites are incredible tools. You can use them to meet someone who lives around the corner or across the country; someone who shares your values, interests, and hobbies; someone seeking a similar level of commitment. You'll learn everything you need to know about online dating, including how to pick a site that's right for you; the difference between mainstream and niche sites; selecting photos that show you at your best; how to make the best use of dating apps, and when and how to meet a match in person. Step 4 is detailed, specific, and includes lots of online dating secrets that will help you maximize success and minimize disappointments.

Step 5: EMBRACE YOUR FUTURE

Embark on Your Personal 60-Day Dating Action Plan

Setting a goal is the best way to convert a dating dream into tangible results, so in Step 5 you'll do just that. Your 60-Day Dating Challenge is a detailed, action-based plan with specific activities you'll complete on a daily and weekly basis. It includes IRL (in real life) activities, such as going on eight first dates, attending singles' and speed-dating events, meetup groups, and non-dating events, as well as IDL (in digital life) goals, like signing up for mainstream and niche dating sites and a mobile dating app, and responding to a designated number of potential dates. This step is all about you and your commitment to dating again to maximize the joy in your life. And your resilience, drive, and desire to love again will propel you to the finish line. Step 5 shows you that you have everything it takes to date successfully and amazingly. Remember, you've got to be in it to win it!

Your success is my greatest pleasure. It's my hope that this book will help you return to dating with joy, enthusiasm, and optimism. May all your dreams come true!

The space in which we live should be for the person we are becoming now, not for the person we were in the past.

—MARIE KONDO,
*THE LIFE-CHANGING MAGIC
OF TIDYING UP*

DECLUTTER:
Adjust to Life after a Breakup

It's over. Your heart is broken. Your head is spinning. Your stomach is turned inside out. You are in a state of denial and disbelief. Why did this happen? You are in a daze and feel paralyzed. The tears start flowing and then you are sobbing uncontrollably. You are inconsolable and don't know what to do.

Does this sound familiar? Believe me when I say: *You will be okay. You will be happy. And you will survive this. I promise.*

I'll be repeating this mantra throughout this book to help keep you focused. Hold onto it as you read this chapter. You may spend quite a bit of time grieving, and you may have some rough days, but that's all right. I will not let you fall apart. It's okay—have a mini meltdown, but then get to work.

Beginning on your Date of Breakup (DOB), you must believe that breakups happen because one of you did not want the relationship or marriage to last forever. It would not have ended if it were fixable.

Say it aloud slowly. Write it down. Commit it to memory.

Breakups turn your life upside down regardless of the circumstances. If you were dumped, the pain is especially agonizing. In fact, in a 2010 study, researchers at the State University of New York at Stony Brook discovered that being rejected is similar, in some ways, to going through withdrawal from a cocaine addiction: MRI findings showed that cocaine craving and romantic rejection share similar brain images. The pain of rejection is so intense because you were "addicted" to the relationship: Once this connection has been severed, you experience relationship withdrawal, which is a shock to your system.

If you were the one who ended things, your road to recovery will be easier because you had some say in the relationship's demise—though you may still agonize over whether calling it quits was the right decision. Still, this doesn't mean you're not grieving, too.

Either way, the bottom line is that the end of a relationship can feel like a living death—especially in the first few days.

Your Breakup Survival Kit

Don't panic: I will help you through this.

Whether you'd seen the writing on the wall or the breakup came without warning, hearing "We're done" is always a devastating shock to your system.

What do you do now? Work on the most important relationship you'll ever have. You'll be with this person for the rest of your life, for better or worse. No, not your ex; it's not your next love; and it's not your rebound relationship. It's YOU. If that makes you feel teary and tender, let the tears flow. I'm here to guide you, support you, and give you your marching orders for the next few days. Together we'll get through this as quickly and easily as possible.

Here's how to start.

Your Lifelines

How to Get Through the First Three Days Post-Breakup

The following activities are designed to ease your pain and promote healing. Even if you are way past the first seventy-two hours post-breakup, they're comforting any time you feel like you're slipping backward. Refer to these as often as you need to.

HEAD LIFELINES

- Remind yourself that everyone goes through losses.
- Focus only on each moment, each hour, each day.
- Distract yourself with mindless TV or a funny movie.

HEART LIFELINES

- Write down your feelings.
- Hug someone who loves you.
- Ask a friend to tell you that you will survive this.

SPIRIT LIFELINES

- Allow yourself to feel.
- Listen to music.
- Meditate.

BODY LIFELINES

- Eat something you love.
- Sleep or rest.
- Take a walk.

Post-Breakup Don'ts: Six Things You'll Quickly Regret

These lifelines are part of the healing process. But don't mistake this for having carte blanche to do whatever you want. There are a few important post-breakup Don'ts—and these are especially important if your breakup happened recently. They're listed here, and I ask that you stick to them. (Trust me: This is for your own good.)

✖ Don't call your ex.

✖ Don't email your ex.

✖ Don't check your ex's social media activity.

✖ Don't take drugs.

✖ Don't drink alcohol.

✖ Don't self-medicate with pills.

It's pretty short, but it's vital that you follow this Don'ts list to the letter. The first three activities on this list will slow—or even undo—the healing process, and engaging in the last three may cause you harm. I know, I know: You *really* want a glass of Chardonnay, but one easily leads to two, and then to—well, eight. And that'll just make you feel worse. So steer clear of all of the Don'ts.

Who Am I?

funny, smart, trendy, adorable, organized, compassionate, clever, caring, fit, helpful, honest, courageous, sexy, terrific, optimistic, candid, insightful, creative, energetic, charming, handy, awesome

Instead, grab your favorite pen. It's time for a quick, fun brainstorming session that puts the focus back on *you*.

Top Ten Fabulous Things about Me

> Breakups happen because one of you did not want the relationship or marriage to last forever. It would not have ended if it were fixable.

It's time to list the top ten positive adjectives that describe you. Why? Feeling good about yourself—and affirming how great you are—is a huge and necessary first step. And it's not enough to do this in your head: You need to see it on paper. I know this is hard to do when your self-esteem is at rock bottom. Take a deep breath, exhale, and give it a shot. If you're struggling to tap into your positive qualities—which is perfectly normal at this time—imagine how your friends and family would describe you, or think of how you felt about yourself Before the Breakup (BTB). On the left are some examples to get you started. Which ones resonate with you? Of course, you can (and should) add your own, too!

THE RULES

Like all games, this one has rules:

- Toot your own horn!
- Don't be shy.
- Don't obsess—just write down what comes to mind.
- Smile as you write.
- Stick to a ten-minute time limit.
- Set your stopwatch.
- No tears (and no wine, please).
- Ready, set, go!

Now that you're done writing, it's time to talk to yourself. (I know: You think I'm crazy.) Look in the mirror as you go through your list and say each adjective aloud. Look yourself in the eye and tell yourself, "I'm _____ ." Say it like you mean it. Then, say it again—like you *really* mean it. Reinforcement is crucial. You might feel a little silly at first, but that's okay.

Congratulations! You've just taken the first steps toward feeling better and moving on!

10 Fabulous Things About Me

1. _____
2. _____
3. _____
4. _____
5. _____
6. _____
7. _____
8. _____
9. _____
10. _____

5 Stages of Grief

1. DENIAL

2. ANGER

3. BARGAINING

4. DEPRESSION

5. ACCEPTANCE

» Dr. Elisabeth Kübler-Ross's five stages of grief serve as a useful
framework for understanding how we heal after a breakup.

Understanding the Stages of Grief after a Breakup

Now the real work begins.

When you reach Day 4, it's time to work on your healing and recovery. I know you're ready for the challenge—and if you're afraid you might not be—well, fake it till you make it, as the saying goes.

My clients always ask, "When will the pain subside? When will I stop thinking about him every second? When will the tears stop? Why don't I care about the positive things happening in my life and around me?" There is no easy answer to these questions because there's no set template for breakup recovery that applies to every person or every breakup. But what you *can* do is understand your grieving process better. You can't rush healing, but you can nurture it so it doesn't take over your life.

That's right. I said grieving process. Many of us think that "grief" refers only to death, but the truth is that grieving is a part of any loss. Dr. Elisabeth Kübler-Ross, author of *On Death and Dying* (1969), identified five stages in the grief process—originally written within the context of a terminal illness diagnosis. However, they apply whenever we experience a loss—of a person, a job, a dream, or a relationship.

These progressive stages help you identify your feelings and responses to your sorrow and grief—although some take longer than others. The more you know and appreciate what is happening to you, the more in control you are, and the less anxious you'll be when you experience these emotions.

One of the most important gifts these five stages can give you is reassurance. It's comforting to know you are not losing your mind—although you might feel like it!—and that all of this is normal. For instance, Sherry told me about a breakup that took her by surprise. She said, "I thought I was losing my mind: one minute I thought this was only a bad dream, and the next minute I was crying hysterically because I knew he was never coming back. I thought there was something wrong with me, only to learn that this is so common after a breakup."

I do believe that time is a great healer, but time alone can't heal all wounds. Instead, time allows you to feel the pain and experience the gamut of emotions—and perhaps these are emotions you never thought you were capable of feeling or expressing. When you allow yourself, over time, to go through this pain and sorrow, you are truly on your way to healing.

Healing might take two months—or it might take twelve months. The amount of time is less important than what you learn during this process. For now, take a deep breath and read on as we explore Kübler-Ross's five stages of grief.

Stage 1: Denial

You're probably pretty familiar with this already: You're in a state of shock and disbelief. You're dazed, frozen, numb, and disoriented because you are traumatized. You pretend nothing has happened, and act as if nothing has changed.

Think of denial as your coziest pair of sweats; your softest sweater; or your warmest, heaviest blanket. Denial protects your heart and mind from the cruel reality of your loss. It only allows you to feel as much pain as you can handle. Denial is your safety net, but please don't let it take control of your life. Don't live in a dream world. You can face the truth. You have to face it—because you don't want to get stuck here. Why? Because, as you begin to believe and accept that your partner is gone, you are actually beginning the healing process. Once you allow it to sink in, emotions flow, and that's all to the good. I know you feel terrible right now, but this is the beginning of your new normal. Hang in there. It does get better. I promise!

Wait—the new normal? Hold the phone. I'm not saying these feelings will never go away. What I am saying is that your recovery starts now. Denial is part of the process.

You will be okay. You will survive. You will be happy.

Stage 2: Anger

"Who the hell does he think he is?"

The volcano is erupting. You can't contain your anger. You are outraged at the way he handled the breakup. "He wasted the best years of my life!" you scream. You want to rip his heart out.

This is the phase in which badmouthing your ex is all you want to do. You tell anyone who will listen—your friends, hairdresser, neighbors, letter carrier, the barista at the coffee shop—even complete strangers. You rattle on ad nauseum, telling them that the man you were living with was the biggest narcissist; a selfish, cheap bastard who should burn in hell for walking out on you two weeks after you lost your job.

At home, you find yourself ripping up photos of him and sending him vile texts and emails because you don't know what to do with your anger. You may even be angry at yourself for not paying attention to the warning signs. Lashing out gives you an immediate feeling of relief—which, sadly, vanishes soon afterward.

Anger can be a good thing. When you're in denial, you can't admit the anger you feel. (Remember, not that long ago you believed that the phone would ring and he'd tell you he made a terrible mistake and wanted you back.) Feeling anger means you've taken your first step toward accepting that it's over. Expressing your anger is healthy. Keeping anger inside will destroy you physically and emotionally: You might suffer from headaches or stomachaches, poor sleep, cloudy thinking, stress, and anxiety.

Anger also allows you to stand up for yourself and begin to regain your self-confidence. Anger can help you regain control of your life, so it's time to celebrate your progress.

Let's get real for a moment. Life is not fair, and there are no lifetime warranties against a broken heart. So, what's an awe-inspiring, cool, brainy woman like you to do? What good can come from taking your anger out on him? Aren't you better than that?

Go ahead—think, dream, and plan all the vindictive, vengeful things you want to do to get back at him for hurting you. But the operative word here is *think*. **Don't act**. It won't be worth the fleeting feeling of victory you imagine you'll experience. If you do something to cause him harm, your actions will haunt and plague you for a long, long time. One more time: It's not worth it.

You will be okay. You will survive. You will be happy.

HOW TO HANDLE ANGER IN A POSITIVE WAY

Anger can be dangerous, but it can be handled in a productive way. The following are some Dos and Don'ts for when you're feeling especially wrathful.

DO NOT:

- Log in or hack into his social media accounts to view or alter them.
- Badmouth him indiscriminately, verbally or on social media.
- Damage or destroy his belongings, even if they're still in your possession.
- Sabotage his current or future relationships.
- Try to ruin his life.

DO:

- Take a social media vacation.
- Feel your anger: Shout it out, talk it out, or write it out.
- Box up his stuff, mail it, or hide it away.
- Focus on your own healing; the sweetest revenge is your own happiness.

Stage 3: Bargaining

You'll do anything to put a screeching halt to the breakup. You promise not to do any of the things that drove your ex crazy—waking up way too early on the weekends; going out with friends he despised; not walking the dog; avoiding her overbearing sister. You swear that if you get just one more chance, you will never be jealous, nag, or force him to go to any business dinners with you ever again.

You go over everything that went on during your relationship and say, "If only I had been more understanding. If only I hadn't been so focused on school. If only I were prettier, or thinner, this never would have happened." You question every decision you made, trying to figure out how to reverse the ones that went wrong. You desperately want to rewrite the script of your relationship.

Ultimately, you can't transform the past. It is time to say our mantra aloud: I will be okay. I will survive. I will be happy. I want you to say it three times. Do not whisper. Say it like you mean it. Go in your car and close the windows and say it. Go into the bathroom and run the water and say it. Blast some music while you say it. Go wherever you have to go, and say it like you mean it. And remember:

The relationship would not have ended if both of us wanted it to last forever or if it were fixable.

Now it's time to do some work. Answer the following questions by writing down your answers. (Don't do this in your head: It's important to put your thoughts on paper.)

Make three lists:

1. The things you wish you did **not do** while you were together.
2. The things you wish you did **more of** while you were together.
3. The things you wish you did **less of** while you were together.

It is vital to do this soul-searching while you can still accurately and honestly recall what you "wish" you had done differently. Put your completed list in a safe place.

Three to six months later, take a look at what you wrote. It will be like revisiting a miniature time capsule to see how far you've come. Or, if you still wish you had done things differently, hold onto those thoughts for when you're dating a fabulous guy. These will be useful lessons for future relationships.

If you look at these notes six months from now and realize the problems were about quirks, misunderstandings, or incompatible traits, it will simply confirm what you already know:

The relationship would not have ended if both of us wanted it to last forever or if it were fixable.

My Three Lists

1. If only I did not do the following:

_____
_____
_____
_____
_____
_____
_____
_____

2. If only I did more of the following:

_____
_____
_____
_____
_____
_____
_____

3. If only I did less of the following:

_____
_____
_____
_____
_____
_____
_____
_____

Stage 4: Depression

Welcome to the worst phase of the process. The good news, though, is that you're in the home stretch. You have to believe that your pain, anguish, and grief will pass—because it will.

The most inescapable, incapacitating feeling during this phase is hopelessness. Meghan, a client of mine, described this stage as "feeling that nothing will ever be good again: I will never, ever have a happy life." During this stage your new best friends may be your bed, TV, the local deli, and the frozen yogurt store—the one that features thirty-six toppings. You get your mail only because your mailbox is stuffed to the brim, and you only listen to your voice mail messages because your voice mailbox is full. You feel apathetic and exhausted from doing nothing. Time just stands still. Every day feels like an eternity. You keep repeating the same negative thoughts over and over: I will never get over him. I can't snap out of this. I will never be happy.

All of what you're feeling is a natural, normal response to a broken heart. Try not to pressure yourself to "just snap out of it"—after all, you don't have an on/off switch when it comes to sadness. There is no magical eraser that can wipe away your feelings of isolation, loneliness, misery, and heartache. Still, continuous negative thoughts will only torment you and prolong your suffering.

Healing your heart is possible only when you feel the depth of your sadness. It is your body's way of getting ready for the last stage in the grieving process.

Are You Depressed?

Check the Yes box for statements you feel are true and the No box for statements you feel are false.

YES NO

☐ ☐ I eat properly.

☐ ☐ I get enough sleep.

☐ ☐ I get some exercise.

☐ ☐ I feel in control of my emotions.

☐ ☐ I shower/bathe regularly.

☐ ☐ I go to work regularly and on time.

☐ ☐ I pay my bills on time.

☐ ☐ I cook my own meals, for the most part.

☐ ☐ I keep my home relatively clean.

☐ ☐ My kids will be fine (if you have kids).

☐ ☐ I have enough money to live on.

☐ ☐ I pay attention to my appearance.

☐ ☐ I accept social invitations.

☐ ☐ I can focus on tasks that need my attention.

☐ ☐ I meet deadlines at work.

☐ ☐ I am friendly with colleagues and customers.

☐ ☐ I know I will find love again.

☐ ☐ I can meet another partner who makes me happy.

Review the items you checked "No." These are the areas that need attention and healing now.

Now, take another look at the checklist. For which "symptoms" did you check the No box? Write them into the following list—then copy your list onto sticky notes. Place the sticky notes in prominent places—such as on your fridge, your cell phone, your desk, or your locker. That way you'll see them often throughout the day. (Don't skip this step! It's really important.)

What I need to work on:

✔ _____
✔ _____
✔ _____
✔ _____
✔ _____
✔ _____
✔ _____
✔ _____
✔ _____
✔ _____
✔ _____
✔ _____
✔ _____
✔ _____
✔ _____
✔ _____

Now write an action plan for the next month for each issue you identified. For instance, let's say you checked off "not exercising" and "binging on food." Your plan might look like this:

✘ **Not exercising**

✔ I will walk ten minutes a day.

✔ I will take the stairs whenever I can.

✘ **Binging on food**

✔ I will get rid of all my junk food.

✔ I will allow myself one treat per day.

✔ I will not buy foods that I know I'll binge on.

At the end of the month, review your progress and revise as needed. Continue working on areas that are still problematic.

You will be okay. You will survive. You will be happy. I promise.

Stage 5: Acceptance

You love that the day is sunny. You laugh at the sitcom on TV. You can go hours, even days, without thinking about your ex. The bitterness has turned to indifference; the anger has been exchanged for forgiveness; and the loneliness has been replaced with activity—everything you had forgotten you loved doing. These days, if you cry, your tears are happy ones because you made it to home plate—you've accepted that it's over and done. You know that a wonderful life awaits you, and you're ready to embrace it.

You didn't get here by magic. It took a lot of hard work, patience, and stamina. So it's time to honor that by sending yourself a thank you note—for not giving in, not giving up, and believing in yourself. You've graduated with honors.

I really want you to write a thank you note to yourself! Need a sample? On the right is a letter that Heidi wrote to herself after her fiancé broke off their engagement six weeks before the wedding because he was secretly engaged to another woman.

During this time, it's important to thank others, too. When you're going through a divorce or breakup, it's easy to become completely self-absorbed and focused only on your needs—often at the neglect and expense of the people on whom you rely most. Now is the perfect time to express your gratitude to the people who were always in your corner, called you daily, took you out to dinner, helped you with your kids, gave you a shoulder to cry

Thank you so much for helping me get through this. I am so grateful that you never gave up on me and encouraged me to express my feelings and pushed me to get out of bed when I did not want to. I love you for everything you did, even pleading with me to see a therapist and join a support group. You never gave up on me and helped me realize that there is a light at the end of the tunnel. Without you, I never would have been able to survive.

With love and appreciation,

Heidi

on, and just let you be. So, make a list of everyone you want to thank; then handwrite a note to each person to say how instrumental his or her love and support was to your healing.

You can finally let out a huge sigh of relief. Life doesn't hurt the way it did before. It's amazing how it happens: You wake up one day and your energy is back; you care what you look like; and you're finally ready to let go of all the pain, anger, disappointment, and regret. Congratulations! You feel like yourself again, and that feels fabulous.

Will you ever feel sad again? Absolutely–but it won't define you, and it won't consume you. You have made peace with the past and are excited to live life the way you want.

You HAVE survived, you ARE okay, you ARE happy.

Remember, the stages of grief don't come in neatly wrapped packages. They don't happen in isolation, and they don't always follow a straight line. You won't necessarily check one off the list, then move on to the next stage. But staying stuck will prevent you from living the happy life you deserve and want. You only have one shot at life, so don't waste your time:

- Pining away for someone who doesn't want you–you deserve to be with someone who wants you totally and completely.

- Being consumed with negativity that takes over your life.

- Feeling so sorry for yourself that it is impossible to move on.

- Holding on to false hope that if you wish hard enough, he'll come back.

PLACING TIME LIMITS ON GRIEF

Can you really set a deadline for grieving? Yes! If you keep putting off getting your life back, I suggest you do what Maddyn did. "My husband and I married and divorced twice," she told me. "I lost thirty pounds after our final divorce because I couldn't keep anything down. I was a total disaster, brokenhearted. I thought my life was over. I had a ten-year-old daughter for whom I was totally responsible since I was the only parent around: My ex moved 500 miles away. The divorce was in May. I gave myself until September to get back out into the world. On September 1, I told myself I had to get my life back; on Labor Day, I posted a profile on an online dating site. I am eternally grateful that I set a grief target date. It worked and I am so happy—happier than I have ever been in my life."

The Value of Decluttering

For most of us, "decluttering" refers to the dreaded task of getting rid of papers, clothing, and other stuff that's taking up our precious space. Although we often don't want to part with these things, we pay a huge price for keeping them: our homes are a mess; we can never find what we want when we need it; and we always feel disorganized. We hold on to our stuff for many reasons. We think we might need it someday; we may have an emotional connection to it; or we feel that letting go is just too hard and painful.

The same thing is true when it comes to breakups. The aftermath of a breakup can leave you with shattered dreams, emotionally charged memories, physical reminders of your ex, and unhealthy attachments. Holding on to them for dear life is agonizing—and worse, it's damaging. Until you let all this baggage go, it'll only delay your healing and happiness.

So this is the perfect time to do some spring-cleaning. Imagine you're cleaning out your relationship "house," opening up your heart and life with a fresh new start. Visualize taking a broom in hand and sweeping out the person who broke your heart. Once you discard the dreams of what "could have" or "should have" been, you'll open yourself to love and happiness. In letting go, you help yourself move toward a place of peace and acceptance—and once you get there, you'll be rewarded with an amazing feeling of freedom and exhilaration. As you sift through the emotional and physical reminders of your ex, your task is to detach and discard and to

10 WAYS TO DECLUTTER YOUR DATING LIFE

1. Disconnect from Your Ex
2. Keep a Journal
3. Ask for Help
4. Connect with Friends
5. Make Plans, Keep Busy, and Establish a Routine
6. Take Care of Your Body
7. Declutter—Literally!
8. Refuse the Rebound Relationship
9. Escape into Your Job
10. Give of Yourself to Someone Who Needs You

visualize what you want the next chapter of your life to look like.

Here's a quick rundown of how to detach, discard, and visualize:

Disconnect from your ex. Remove yourself from his social media presence; delete texts, emails, and photos, and eliminate all contact.

🕐 Do this right away after your breakup or divorce.

Journal your moods, thoughts, beliefs, feelings, and attitudes so you can release the clutter from your mind and free your heart from the pain of your breakup. (Putting your thoughts and feelings on paper helps process them and facilitates closure.)

🕐 Begin the date of your breakup. Continue journaling until you feel you don't need it anymore.

Flex your muscles—the muscles that allow you to reach out to others, that is. Ask for help—join a support group or see a therapist.

🕐 Reach out whenever you need help from others who are going through a breakup, or when you want to talk about your feelings with a professional.

Make room in your life for friends, routines, plans, exercise, your job, and for giving back to your community.

🕐 Begin as soon as you feel ready. Adding joy to your life lessens the hurt.

Reorganize and rejuvenate your home. Give your bedroom a makeover; think of it as your private retreat. Transform your living space into a special place of comfort and support.

🕐 Begin as soon as possible after your breakup or divorce.

Beware of the rebound. Rebound relationships may not be good for you right now.

🕐 Be mindful from the date of your breakup or divorce until the end of Step 1 (see page 45).

Now is the time to clear the emotional mess out of your life and replace it with fresh, sparkling, spotless, unsoiled thoughts and feelings. This won't happen overnight, but the sooner you start the faster you will heal and (Yes!) be happy again. Let's get going.

> » Decluttering is about reducing the distractions and unhappy memories in your life and embracing what brings you joy.

10 Ways to Make a Clean Break, Stop Feeling Paralyzed & Know Yourself Better

❶ Disconnect from Your Ex

Okay: I know you don't want to do this. You want to hug that beautiful photo of the two of you smiling; you want to bury your face in the sweater he left behind to catch the scent of his cologne; you want to wear every piece of jewelry he ever gave you; and you treasure all the loving cards, texts, and emails ever sent.

I GET IT.

If you must, you can do all of these things for ninety-six hours after the breakup—but that's it. After day four, you need to go cold turkey. And the best way to detach is to disengage. This is the hardest part of your breakup recovery, but it's vital to getting on with the rest of your life.

So, how's a smart, sophisticated, feisty gal like you gonna cut the cord?

DETOX FROM SOCIAL MEDIA

I asked Julianna to tell me what the most important tool in her Breakup Survival Kit was—the one that really helped ease the pain for her. She explained, "I was with Jared for six years. I loved him with my heart and soul. After he told me we were done, I was in the fetal position on my living room floor, sobbing for what felt like hours. Within the next forty-eight hours, I did what was infinitely more difficult than quitting smoking: I cut off all social media contact. EVERYTHING. I unfriended, deleted, untagged, and unfollowed. I was obsessed with being disconnected, because deep down, in the depths of my soul, I knew that it had to be this way. It was the BEST thing I ever did."

You know the cliché that claims that ignorance is bliss? Well, it's absolutely true during your worst breakup moments. Wondering what your ex is doing is so much better than knowing the details. (Yes, really.) When you know the details, you're pulling the scab off the wound repeatedly—and you're re-injuring your heart.

It's tempting to think that if you stay connected on social media, you'll "know the whole story" about what he's doing and who he's doing it with. On the contrary: You'll only get snippets of information, and your imagination will be your worst enemy.

DELETE TEXTS AND EMAILS

I'm serious. It's over. Holding onto loving texts and emails just lends a false sense of security. The fact is, he's gone and not coming back. So there is no purpose to keeping them. If you don't press delete, you are traumatizing yourself every time you look at those loving words—just as you would if you kept on checking his social media profiles. You deserve better.

Antoinette told me, "I tried my hardest to delete Jeff's emails, but I just couldn't—or, should I say, wouldn't. I copied the ones that meant the most to me out of the 421 emails I had from him. Then I put them in a box in my storage unit, which is in the basement of my apartment building. It was the best I could do."

This is what I call tough self-love. Getting rid of reminders of "what was" is fundamental to letting go and moving on. I know how grueling this is, but the only person that can help you with this one is YOU! When you delete the negativity of the past, it enables you to get ready for the love-filled future that awaits you. (I promise!)

PURGE THE PHOTOS

They're everywhere—your phone, your tablet, the walls, your drawers, and your desk.

But they need to be out of your sight, and there are no ifs, ands, or buts about this. So let me outline your choices. Press delete; burn them; rip them up; toss them in the garbage; put them in the shredder; or ask a friend to hide them in your house.

You do have one other option. You could give *all* your photos (digital and paper) to a trusted friend. Whew, right? Not so fast. Your photos will be returned to you in two years. By then, they'll have little or no meaning to you.

Don't believe me? During one of my Breakup Survival Workshops, Erica told the group that she did not want to part with a single photo, and that she would never take my advice about destroying all the memories. But Jody, another workshop member, said, "The only thing you can do to move on is to rid yourself of the memories."

The two women made a bet: Jody told Erica that she would safeguard all her photos for two years. If, during those two years, Erica did not ask for the pictures, Jody would hand deliver them to her at the end of that time. A year and a half later, Erica told Jody that she'd met the man of her dreams, and asked her to dump the photos. She was moving in with her new boyfriend, and the old memories had no place in her new life. Can you believe it?

If you have kids, removing photos may feel even more difficult, but it's still doable. For example, Amy couldn't bear to look at any pictures of her ex-husband. She said, "I had to make some tough choices, because my two kids, ages eleven and fifteen, live with me. We talked about it and I told them that I was taking down our wedding pictures and the photos of family vacations that included my ex. But I told them that they could keep them in their rooms if they wanted to."

Getting rid of photos of your ex is cathartic and cleansing. After all, when "he" is in your face 24/7, you risk replaying all of the what-if's over and over. And the anguish of seeing the happy times that once were is far worse than feeling the emptiness of not seeing his photos at all.

FOLLOW THE 90-DAY "NO-CONTACT" RULE

The best way to free yourself from the power your ex has over you is to sever all contact with him. This might seem impossible, but your cravings, dependence, and obsession with your lost love will disappear—I promise—if you follow the 90-Day Rule of Absolutely No Contact Whatsoever.

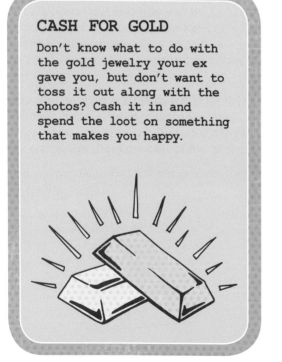

CASH FOR GOLD

Don't know what to do with the gold jewelry your ex gave you, but don't want to toss it out along with the photos? Cash it in and spend the loot on something that makes you happy.

Now, I understand that if you have kids together (or other shared concerns such as a business), or if you go to the same school or live in the same building, some contact may be unavoidable. Stay tuned: I'll show you how to get through that. But first, let's define "no contact," just so we're clear about what it means:

The Eleven No-Contact Rules

1. Do not call your ex.
2. Do not call your ex and hang up.
3. Do not leave messages on your ex's phone(s).
4. Do not text your ex.
5. Do not email your ex.
6. Do not drive past your ex's house.
7. Do not ask your ex's friends or family about him.
8. Do not send your ex anything via the mail, UPS, FedEx, etc.
9. Do not hang out at your ex's favorite spots.
10. Do not show up at your ex's job.
11. Do not snoop on your ex on social media.

Remember, you are in charge of your life—even if resisting contact feels unbearable. Sometimes your "magical thinking" gets activated, and you imagine that your aching heart would feel better if only you could see him, or hear his voice, just one more time. But it won't. So, to speed your healing and recovery, I want you to sign this contract with yourself.

No-Contact Rules

Please **rewrite** each No-Contact Rule on the blank line beneath it. Then sign and date the contract in the space provided.

1. I will not call my ex.

   _____

2. I will not call my ex and hang up.

   _____

3. I will not leave messages on my ex's phone(s).

   _____

4. I will not text my ex.

   _____

5. I will not email my ex.

   _____

6. I will not drive past my ex's house.

   _____

7. I will not ask my ex's friends or family about him.

   _____

8. I will not send my ex anything via the mail, UPS, FedEx, etc.

   _____

9. I will not hang out at my ex's favorite spots.

   _____

10. I will not show up at my ex's place of work.

    _____

11. I will not snoop on my ex on social media.

    _____

_____   _____

Signature   Date

Now that we've established that you will not contact your ex, how do you manage the "No-contact" Rule if you have to see him due to kids, work, school, or your living situation?

I wish I had a foolproof method for handling this one. Here are the facts:

- It's not going to be simple or easy. Accept this.

- Replace in-person contact with text, email, or phone contact as much as possible.

- Don't use your kids as an excuse for contact. (For example, maybe your daughter is in a school play, and you arrive early to "save a seat" for your ex so you can sit next to him and spend time with him. This will not help your healing process. Support your daughter but sit separately.)

- Remember, your children's well-being is your priority. If and when you have to see each other, make it as easy and pleasant as possible for the kids. For their sakes, you have to.

Keep contact brief, to the point, and drama free. Stick to a specific focus: your kids, the business, the house, etc.

If contact with your ex is unavoidable, treat this contact like a business endeavor. Your boundaries with your customers, clients, or associates would be well defined, as they should be with your ex. To that end, here are some "business guidelines" to follow with your ex: No yelling, denigrating, bullying, name-calling, talking behind his back, showing up uninvited, or calling at all hours of the day or night just because you want to! Got it?

❷ Keep a Journal: Your Breakup Chronicles

The British scholarly journal *Advances in Psychiatric Treatment* reports some great outcomes of putting your thoughts and feelings on paper. The winners are "improved mood" (and goodness knows we all need that when we're recovering from a breakup); "feelings of greater psychological well-being" (also known—in my book, at least—as feeling happier and better); and "fewer stress-related visits to the doctor" (otherwise known as better health). Writing down your thoughts and feelings has other benefits, too:

- It releases your emotions.
- It's validating.
- You gain insight from seeing your thoughts and feelings laid out in front of you.
- It allows you to be self-reflective, which leads to increased self-worth.
- It helps you see things in another light.
- It feels good to be honest—it's freeing.
- It helps you process your loss.

So how should you approach your Breakup Chronicles? There are lots of ways to journal. Here are six: Experiment with whichever styles resonate with you.

LET IT FLOW

Write down anything and everything that comes to mind. Don't censor yourself, and don't hold back. After all, you're the only person who will ever read it. Include your feelings, thoughts, fears, dreams, regrets, and your happiest and saddest times. Make sure to include the day, date, and time for each entry: Later, when you review your entries, it'll be helpful for charting your ups and downs, the progression of your healing, and any patterns that might emerge. For example, every Friday afternoon you might feel bursts of anxiety and sadness, or on Monday mornings, you might notice that you feel relieved.

This technique works best if you are consumed with conflicting emotions, confusion, and general misery. It's also a tremendous help in the very early stages of a breakup, since this is when you feel like your life has just been turned upside down and inside out. You need a safety valve, so the "Let it Flow" technique is just what the Breakup Doctor (That's me!) ordered.

QUESTION-AND-ANSWER JOURNAL

If you want to write about your breakup but don't know where to start, brainstorm and write down questions that you want answers to—as many as you can think of. Pick a question from your list to use as a starting point. Or, you can begin with a single question, and use it as a springboard for additional questions. This approach works especially well if you are seeking clarity or closure.

If coming up with questions seems too daunting, never fear: Here are a few that will help you generate some of your own questions. There are no rules here: Answer any or all of the questions listed. They'll give your thoughts some structure.

- What do I miss most about my ex?
- What is now possible for me that wasn't possible when I was with my ex?
- Why did we break up?
- What part did I play in the demise of the relationship?
- What did I hate about my ex?
- Why am I better off without him or her?

What I love most about this approach is that you'll feel a sense of completion with each question you answer. It also lets you reflect on the breakup in small doses, since you come up with your own questions. It's great if structure and order is what you need.

WRITE A LETTER TO YOUR EX

Closure is often hard to get when a breakup occurs. But writing a letter to your ex can help. It allows you to disclose your most closely held secrets, regrets, or words of affection. It offers catharsis to your pent-up feelings. If you feel like you're bursting at the seams with your emotions, this technique may be the perfect outlet.

In it, you get to state your closing argument, and write the final chapter of your breakup. One caveat: The Breakup Doctor (That's me!) has prescribed this remedy for you and only you. So this letter is for your eyes only and should never actually be sent to your ex. (I'm just looking out for you.)

> Clutter is not just the stuff on your floor. It's anything that stands between you and the life you want to be living.
>
> PETER WALSH

YOUR HEALING JOURNAL

For some people, the most beneficial journal entries are the ones that don't dwell on the breakup, the sadness, the anger, or the heartache. The focus of the healing journal is to chronicle what you're doing to move on with your life. In it, you list what you're actively doing to make your life better, more productive, and more focused on the future.

But before you think this is a free-for-all, here are the rules for the healing journal:

The Dos

✔ Write at least one entry each day.

✔ The tone of the entry must be positive. (Yes, you can find something positive to write about every day.)

✔ Write down anything you did that felt uplifting or helpful–getting out of bed; reading the mail; going out with an old friend; going to a movie.

✔ Write down anything that made you smile, like the softest, cuddliest Labrador puppy who just melts in your arms; the most amazing sunset; your best friend's description of you at karaoke night; or the feeling you had when you found out you got your dream job.

✔ Write down what you did to distract yourself from your grief when it reared its ugly head. For instance, "I told myself to stop thinking about him." "I thought about what I am grateful for." "I told myself I'll get through this." "I went outside." "I turned on the radio." "I went shopping." "I cleaned." "I talked to a coworker."

✔ Write down the length of time you were able to go without thinking about your ex (even if it was only two minutes).

✔ Write down one or two things you did today that you found difficult but were necessary for your healing. For example, "I accomplished everything on my to-do list." "I went out to lunch by myself." "I registered for a support group." "I asked a friend to go to the movies." "I finally told my boss that I'm getting divorced." "I accepted an invitation to my friend's surprise fortieth birthday party."

✔ Write down one thing that you'll do tomorrow that's crucial to your healing. Perhaps, "I will ask a coworker to go to lunch instead of crying at my desk." "I will go food shopping." "I will let my next-door neighbor know that [NAME OF EX] moved out." "I will make the dental appointment that I canceled three times." or "I'm going to buy waterproof mascara."

The Don'ts

✖ No complaining.

✖ No venting.

✖ No tears.

✖ No pity party.

✖ No rehashing, retelling, or repeating the same sob stories over and over.

Your healing journal is very special and meaningful. Although you are crying on the inside, this approach forces you to push beyond the pain, drawing on your resilience and strength in order to start looking ahead and stop wallowing in your grief.

YOUR UGLY AND WICKED JOURNAL

If you find yourself devastated and despondent, grab your pen and let it out. Write down everything that was wrong with your relationship—everything that made you mad, made you cringe, made you feel embarrassed, lonely, sad, furious, betrayed, and downright miserable. When all that emotion goes from your brain to the journal, a "chemical reaction" occurs: It's like opening a bottle of soda. That "fizz" you feel is your "aha!" moment. You finally get it. It's in black and white, right before your eyes. And you can't run away from the truth. I have to confess that I don't have any scientific proof of why this works—but it does. At times we all make excuses and make light of what was actually terribly wrong—but here, you can't sugar coat the facts. You're putting down on paper everything that was malicious, hurtful, cruel, demeaning, humiliating, revolting, and hostile. You are no longer pretending. And while you may find these things embarrassing and uncomfortable to admit, doing so is incredibly liberating and therapeutic.

YOUR GRATITUDE JOURNAL

No matter what's happened to me throughout my life—getting dumped by the love of my life; losing my father in my twenties; my mother's death; being laid off from my job; my breast cancer diagnosis; my husband's prostate cancer diagnosis; the death of my best friend; or getting the worst haircut ever—I always go to a place of gratitude to help me see the light at the end of the tunnel.

To make the most of your gratitude journal, I recommend writing five entries per day, one to two hours before bed for the first week. This structure will get you into the rhythm of writing, and will help you make this a daily habit. After the first week, you can write entries two to three times per week—but ultimately, that's up to you.

Don't forget to include anything and everything that brings you joy—like the restful sleep you had, the delicious leftovers in your refrigerator, or finding your lost remote control. You can also think about people, pets, places, and things. And you can use all your senses, too: "I am grateful that I can see." "I am grateful that I can smell the cookies baking." "I am grateful that I could hug my son." or "I am grateful that I could taste the hot and sour soup." Be creative and artistic: How about including tangible reminders of your joy, like the ticket stub from a great movie or show; a copy of your paid-off credit card bill; your lucky penny; or a favorite photo?

When sadness or loneliness smacks you in the face, pull out your journal and reread everything you're grateful for. Gratitude will pay you back with increased joy, more optimism, improved energy, and renewed feelings of hope. And being grateful every day during your breakup recovery is essential to helping you heal and move on.

> When you allow yourself to go through this necessary pain and sorrow, you are on your way to healing.

❸ Ask for Help

Asking for help is a sign of strength, not weakness. There is no reason to tough it out on your own. You will be amazed at how willing people are to offer their support and help. When your burden is shared, you will feel a huge sense of relief. Here are some places to find help.

SUPPORT OR SELF-HELP GROUPS

There's nothing more comforting than being around others who are in the same boat as you. It's the perfect place to get validation for what you're experiencing; to make new single friends; to seek support and guidance; and to learn coping strategies. Plus, you add structure to your life by committing to showing up on a weekly basis. All to the good!

These groups are led by a trained professional, and usually meet for a designated period of time: say, eight to ten sessions, with one session per week. Many community centers, houses of worship, libraries, and municipal buildings offer support groups for separated and divorced men and women. Here's an example of how support groups can help:

Samantha and her husband relocated from Texas to Delaware. After two years in Delaware, her marriage ended. Feeling alone and terrified, Samantha found a support group for the newly divorced. The group met on Tuesday evenings for eight weeks. Samantha said, "It was the only constant in my life: everything else felt out of control. I met a woman, Tracy, whom I felt so comfortable with. We would meet for coffee during the week. Having a new friend in my life was beyond wonderful. I'm so thankful I joined this group. It was my lifeline."

NOURISH YOUR INQUIRING MIND

Do your research! Read up on what others do when they go through a loss like yours—or ask them. You have already taken a huge step by reading this book and by trying the strategies in it, which are designed to get you through this as quickly and smoothly as possible. So don't be afraid to ask other people what helped them—especially those who are clearly happy and flourishing.

THERAPY

When you're traveling, what do you take with you? Do you show up at the airport with two supersized bags that cost you and arm and a leg to check?

If so, your baggage is ruining your trip! And the same thing applies to your recovery. If your "baggage" is weighing you down, slowing your healing process, and taking up too much space in your life, consider seeing a therapist. It's the best gift you can give yourself. And a therapist who specializes in relationships can help you in so many ways. Here are just a few of the benefits of therapy:

- Therapy helps you take control of your post-breakup life.

- The agenda is focused only on *you: your* needs and *your* future.

- Therapy helps you understand your emotions and the effect they have on your life.

- The therapist will assist you in dealing with the aftermath of your breakup or divorce; in fact, she is trained to do so.

- The therapist provides a safe place in which you can talk about anything.

- The therapist offers techniques for managing stress, grief, and self-defeating behaviors.

- Therapy is the perfect venue for getting advice on helping your kids deal with the pain and difficulties they are experiencing.

Melanie experienced a long, drawn-out divorce. Her husband lived in the basement apartment of their home. After reconciling once, Melanie knew that divorce was no longer a maybe: It was an absolute necessity. She thought that once she got divorced, her life would go back to normal. "Therapy was the most important divorce decision I made," she said. "My therapist was amazing: She listened, she cared, and she didn't let me make excuses or wallow in my self-hatred (I was very good at that). During my eight months of therapy, my confidence soared, and I gained insight into my marriage that I never would have discovered without it. Don't be afraid of it: It's a life changer if you have the right therapist. I interviewed two therapists before I picked the one that felt right for me."

The end of a relationship is traumatic, and some view it as a personal failure. Therapy can help you deal with your feelings, make sense of the end of your relationship, acquire a healthy perspective on the future, and discover what is important to you in a loving partnership.

❹ Connect with Friends

Authentic friends help soothe the pain, wipe away our tears, take us out to dinner when we need company and support, and make us laugh when it seems as if our lives are crumbling before our very eyes. They know just what to say (or not to say!) to make us believe that life will get better. Now is the time to call on your friends. Here are some ways to connect (or reconnect) with friends post-breakup.

GRAB YOUR BREAKUP PALS

To put it simply: You need a breakup pal to be there for you. Who's your breakup pal? Someone you can call when you have the impulse to call your ex; when you can't sleep; or when you pull up at the take-out window of your favorite burger joint, on the verge of supersizing everything. You'll want to "hire" two or three breakup pals to get you through your 90-Day "No-Contact" Rule.

I know what you're thinking: "Hire someone to be my friend?" Here's what I want you to do: Invite two or three friends to lunch. The friends you select should love you, be good listeners, and be willing to be there for you as much as they can. Tell them that you've handpicked them as your breakup pals because of their wisdom and compassion. (Lay it on thick!) Pick a fun place for lunch—and please, pick up the tab. Tell your pals that for the next ninety days, they will act as your superegos, your gurus, your personal advice columnists. Their job is to help you stay on track; to not contact your ex; to be your dinner date when necessary; and to be willing to talk or text at a moment's notice.

Now, *your* job is to hold up your end of the bargain. Call them whenever you need a shoulder to cry on; a friend to kick you in the butt to get you off the pity pot; or a smiling face to go to the movies with. Don't let your pals down. They want to be your pillars of strength, your voices of reason, and your sounding boards.

RECONNECT WITH OLD FRIENDS

I know some of you did not make time for your friends while you were with your ex—because you were too busy, because your ex never liked them, or because, frankly, you just didn't care enough to maintain your friendships. This is a good time to reach out to your "dumped friends." First, you owe them a sincere apology. Next, make a plan to get together and catch up. Then, keep the friendship going; get into a pattern of regular contact. Rekindling friendships will bring joy into your life.

MAKE NEW FRIENDS

If this sounds foreign or scary, take it from me: You can have a whole variety of friends. They are not one size fits all. You need to expand your social circle, so here is a fabulous list of the many kinds of friends you should be looking for:

- **Dinner-date friends.** You both love catching up over leisurely meals—and they can last for hours.
- **Movie/activity friends.** You go to horror movies (or yoga, or art classes) together.

- **Spur-of-the-moment friends.** Suddenly it occurs to you: You're dying for a coffee, or you feel like trying that new wine bar. Call her: You know she'll be there in ten!

- **Fitness friends.** There's nothing better for inspiring you to hit the gym or to go back to the spinning class you abandoned three months ago.

- **Traveling friends.** Finding compatible travel companions can be tricky, so these friends are extra special. Break out of your routine and head off on day trips together or make plans to explore a new city on a weekend.

- **Pour-your-heart-out-to friends.** No such thing as small talk here: deep, soul-searching conversations are *the* order of business when the two of you meet.

- **Shopping friends.** Feel like checking out the sales? Maybe you need a drop-dead gorgeous dress for your friend's thirtieth birthday party, or the perfect outfit for a work conference. He's got impeccable taste, so text him to see if he's free.

- **Telephone friends.** You don't see each other often, but you talk on the phone all the time—and there's always lots to say.

- **Work friends.** You spend eight hours a day—or more—together, so you've bonded and really get each other. Go ahead and talk shop: Share your professional dreams—and your fears and concerns.

FIND YOUR SINGLE SPIRIT GUIDES

Every newly single woman needs a Single Spirit Guide (or Guides). These gals are full of positive energy, understand the sting of a breakup, and know how to make lemonade out of lemons. They enjoy life and have fun being single—but, at the same time, they feel empowered to take control of their love lives. Wallowing, complaining, and feeling sorry for themselves have nothing to do with who they are. Identify yours, and spend time with them frequently.

Doing this meant the world to Juliet, one of my clients. "I was becoming a recluse: going to work, picking up dinner on my way home, eating in front of the TV, and then curling up in bed for hours," she said. "It was getting pretty scary and out of control. I knew I had to make some really drastic changes in my life. I called a few of my single friends: not just any single friends, but the ones who were upbeat, positive, and—yes—even content being single. Don't get me wrong: They all wanted to find 'him,' but they had the best attitude, and were so much fun to be with. I asked them to be my 'Single Spirit Guides,' and told them I wanted to go out with them. We went to a club, danced, and had so much fun. My feet were killing me by the end of the night, but my heart had had a few hours of relief. I hugged my friends, and, with tears in my eyes, said, 'I am so lucky to have you.'"

❺ Make Plans, Keep Busy, and Establish a Routine

Now that you've reconnected with friends, you must make plans to stay connected–and to get yourself into a new, healthy routine. After all, there's nothing worse than isolating yourself at home, ruminating, worrying, crying, sleeping, and engaging in mindless eating. So, jump in the shower, put on your skinny clothes, and get out of the house. It doesn't matter what you do: Go food shopping, meet a friend, run some errands, help a neighbor, go to the mall and window-shop, take a drive, or get away for the weekend.

Whatever you do, the key is to plan ahead. Force yourself to make a plan. Get your calendar out and book activities during the times that are the saddest and most difficult for you. For instance, if you dread the weekends, schedule plans for as much of the weekend as possible. This is your new job–to distract yourself from your sadness and loneliness. Have some fun and take advantage of your freedom: You can now do whatever you want, whenever you want.

If it's your weekend without the kids, relish your newfound freedom rather than being miserable that your ex has the kids. Do things that you can't do when your kids are around. Think of it as precious time that's devoted to you and only you.

And you have to find ways to have social interaction, even if all you want to do is hibernate. Trust me when I say that you have to get up, get out, and get going: You don't have any time to waste! Here's what I suggest:

✔ Don't decline social invitations. I know you don't want to go solo; I know it's a monumental effort to put on a happy face; and I know you're not in the mood for doing these things–but you've got to. Shared social experiences with friends, family, coworkers, or neighbors can be a wonderful way to help you feel connected to other people. They promote a sense of belonging–a feeling that your breakup has snatched away from you. It'll also minimize your loneliness and will distract you from the discomfort of being alone. (There's one exception to the rule, though: You can turn down a social invitation if your ex will be there and you're not ready to be in his presence.)

✔ Book a trip, plan a getaway, be a tourist in your own city, make a brunch reservation, go visit a friend for the weekend, or plan something fun or outrageous! Having something to look forward to is medicine for your soul.

✔ Join a singles' golf league, volunteer at the local food bank, get involved in a cause you're passionate about, take a class–or do anything else that involves interacting with others.

✔ Be the social organizer!–even if you weren't before your breakup. Ask your neighbor to go to the beach; invite your colleagues for a drink after work; go through your contacts and get in touch with three people you haven't seen in a while, make seeing them a priority.

Routines will become one of your lifelines. They give you structure and purpose, and they make each day a little easier because you don't have to think: You just have to do. Here's proof. Nancy told me, "Getting out of bed in the morning, whether or not I had to go to work, was impossible. I was chronically late and running out of plausible excuses. I had to do something—otherwise I was in jeopardy of losing my job, which was my refuge. I work late hours and I am exhausted when I get home. I decided that I would wake up an hour earlier than I had to (can you believe it?) and straighten up my apartment, exercise, or do the prep work for dinner. I needed a reason to get out of bed other than going to work. It wasn't a piece of cake, but I knew that each day I had to accomplish one of those tasks before work. Within two weeks I was never late for work; I had a delicious dinner a few nights a week; and I even fit in some exercise. (Sorry to report that my apartment was still a mess!) I am ecstatic, and it was so simple."

Having new routines, keeping busy, and being proactive in making plans is a structured way of giving your life renewed meaning and hope.

❻ Take Care of Your Body

You only get one body, so treat it with tender loving care! It is so easy to neglect it when you are in the midst of a painful breakup. If your health diminishes, it will make your breakup recovery so much harder. So, do not take your health for granted; take good care of yourself. You will be so glad you did.

GET MOVING

I don't care what you do, but every day you must do something physical. My favorite type of exercise is walking—because the act of putting one foot in front of another is a metaphor for your new beginning. Don't worry about where, when, or how long you need to spend doing it.

If walking doesn't do it for you, do what you love; do what you do best; do what you can; try something new. Exercise is your body's remedy for feeling happier, more energetic, and physically stronger. Go to the gym; take a class; do some gardening; clean the house; go dancing. Come on, you can do it. If you need more ideas, take a look at the list below. Which ones will you do?

☐ Strength training

☐ Running

☐ Yoga

☐ Pilates

☐ Zumba

☐ Bowling

☐ Tennis

☐ Golf

☐ Swimming

☐ Cross-training

☐ Biking

☐ Volleyball

☐ Belly dancing

☐ Martial arts

Now that you've chosen an activity, I want you to write down the what, when, and how. After all, you need a schedule. You can't leave exercise to chance because it'll go straight to the bottom of your to-do list. (I know: I've been there.) So, fill in the blanks below. I've included some examples.

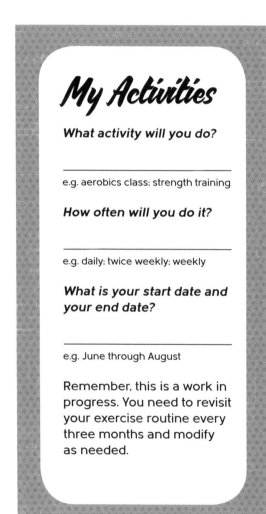

My Activities

What activity will you do?

_____

e.g. aerobics class; strength training

How often will you do it?

_____

e.g. daily; twice weekly; weekly

What is your start date and your end date?

_____

e.g. June through August

Remember, this is a work in progress. You need to revisit your exercise routine every three months and modify as needed.

EAT, SLEEP, AND RELAX

Your body needs you now more than ever. Do not damage it by overeating, binge eating, starving yourself, or filling up on junk food. Lindsey told me how her breakup affected her relationship with food. "I always struggled with my weight," she said. "After my breakup, all I wanted to do was eat. My weight was going through the roof. I joined Weight Watchers, which was a lifesaver because the weekly meetings provided me with support; I was weighed once a week (a curse and a blessing!); and I learned how to eat better. If it wasn't for my breakup, I would never have gotten my weight under control. I have a goal, and that keeps me focused and driven."

Your body will also break down if you are sleep deprived and if you don't relax and recharge your battery. Stephanie struggled with sleeping after her breakup: "I would fall asleep as soon as my head hit the pillow," she said. "At three o'clock in the morning I would awaken, thinking about how lonely and scared I felt about the future. I could not stop the racing thoughts in my head. I tried everything—and then I hit the jackpot. I did anything I hated doing: filing papers, emptying the dishwasher, cleaning out drawers, balancing my checkbook. It was the best 'sleeping pill' I could ever have imagined!"

Relaxing and recharging is so important when your life is filled with stress and anxiety—but it's hard for most of us. We see it as a luxury, a waste of time—and besides, we don't even know how to do it. That's where relaxation techniques come in. They can lower your blood pressure, slow your heart rate, and reduce fatigue. This technique, called progressive relaxation, has worked well for my clients. It helps you experience the difference between tensing your muscles and relaxing them. It's simple, and it takes just five minutes. (If you have more time, even better!) Here's how to do it:

- Start with tensing the muscles in your toes for five seconds; now relax them for thirty seconds. Repeat.

- Move from your toes to your ankles and legs, working your way to the top of your head until you've tensed and released all the muscle groups in your body.

- You'll be amazed at how quickly you feel more relaxed and less stressed!

There are other ways to minimize stress, too. Jill, one of my clients, was so over-scheduled it was impossible for her to find any time to relax—or so she thought. Everything changed after she came down with the worst case of the flu and was forced to relax and take care of herself. She gave herself permission to do nothing until she felt better. Jill realized that relaxing was something she had to schedule, just like everything else in her way-too-busy life. On social media, she heard about an evening yoga class on the beach. It was just what she needed to learn the power of focusing, breathing, and peacefulness.

So here's your prescription from the Breakup Doctor:

✔ Eat well.

✔ Sleep peacefully.

✔ Relax often.

You must make a conscious plan to nurture your body so your heart can heal.

❼ Declutter–Literally!

The fact is, too much stuff is a stress trigger. Let's get rid of some clutter–and start to reorganize and refresh your home. Marni, a client, told me, "I caught my husband Michael cheating; his email was left open and I could not believe my eyes. He'd had a girlfriend for six months and it was only a matter of time before he was going to tell me he wanted a divorce. The details of the emails were revolting, and the betrayal I felt was sickening. You could have told me that my entire family was murdered: That's how devastated I was. Days after Michael moved out I ordered a new bed and comforter, and had 'my bedroom' painted. I rearranged the furniture, got rid of his dresser, and threw out all the sheets we ever slept on. I had to do this, even though money was tight: It was necessary for my sanity. My bedroom was now my safe haven. I was not haunted by Michael."

Like Marni, you'll want to clean up the mess–literally–after your breakup. Here's how:

• **Envision what you want.** During your relationship you shared your space with your ex, even if you didn't live together. Perhaps her needs overshadowed yours, or you always wished you could ditch the uncomfortable couch he treasured. Now you can reclaim all of your space: take over the closet; stash your extra shoes under the bed; or use the dining room table for craft projects. Visualize ways in which you can make your home the perfect space for you–a place that expresses who you truly are.

DECLUTTERING YOUR EMOTIONAL SPACE

Rona, one of my clients, told me how decluttering helped her work through her negative feelings. "My anxiety was out of control. I had so much nervous energy I couldn't sit still," she said. "I needed to channel it, so I embarked on a mission. I cleaned out every closet and drawer in my apartment. I hated every minute of it; it was exhausting. At times I created a total mess and such chaos that it intensified my feelings of being overwhelmed and depressed. When it was done, I felt as if I had literally moved a mountain. It was such a feeling of relief, calm, and order—which hadn't existed in my life after my breakup. I was stunned that I was able to focus on tidying up. It also had a serendipitous effect: My obsessions and ruminations took a vacation! It was the only peaceful time in my day."

- **Remember, decluttering brings clarity.** So don't declutter when you are exhausted, starved, or not feeling well. If your best time of day is before the sun comes up, declutter early in the morning. Whenever you choose to do it, keep in mind that your home should not be a museum or a shrine to your past relationship. It's not good for you. Think of decluttering as a way to help you to go from dwelling on the breakup to moving ahead with your life—instead of overanalyzing everything.

- **Focus on joy.** According to Marie Kondo, a professional organizer and author of the book *The Life-Changing Magic of Tidying Up* (2014), decluttering is based on one simple fact—joy. For example, she suggests organizing by category, starting with clothing because clothes are the least emotionally charged items. As you hold each piece, you are to ask yourself, "Does this bring me joy?" Simple yet very powerful, right? If it does not bring you joy, donate it, give it to a friend, take it to a consignment shop, or ditch it. I've tried this, and it's amazingly freeing. You can use this technique beyond your belongings, too: It can help you make other important life decisions, because joy is such a gut feeling.

- **Try the hangers trick.** Turn all of the hangers in your closet around so they face the opposite direction. After you wear each item, put it back in your closet with the hanger facing forward. After several months you'll see which items of clothing you wore and which ones you didn't. It makes decluttering a breeze!

- **Find relief.** Purging the reminders of your ex will bring you relief and lighten your emotional load. Don't be afraid to remove reminders: If you have a dozen bars of her favorite soap, donate them to a homeless shelter. Or, dump his old tee shirts—the ones you rescued to wear as PJs. And that awful necklace he got you? Give it away! Nostalgia is not your friend.

You know that feeling you get when you let out a huge sigh of relief? That's just what will happen at the end of this process, because decluttering your living space declutters your emotional space. You won't feel like a hostage in your own house. You are in control.

❽ Refuse the Rebound Relationship

After your breakup it can be tempting to jump right into the nearest, most convenient relationship—also known as a rebound relationship. Doing this haphazardly is almost always a bad idea. It just happens without warning, and it's rarely intentional. You are single again, with a bleeding heart: You feel as if you were just punched in the stomach and are gasping for air. And there he is—the anesthetic for your pain. You don't mean to fall head over heels for him, but you can't stop yourself. He is everything your ex wasn't. You feel alive, wanted, and suddenly you don't hurt so much. What could be better?

When a client says something along those lines to me, I take a deep breath and issue a few warnings:

- **Detach and reflect.** You need to take time to detach and reflect on the relationship you had with your ex. How about doing a relationship autopsy and identifying the part you played in the relationship's end? Be honest with yourself and figure out what role you played—otherwise you'll repeat the same mistakes over and over in a vicious cycle.

> When you move too quickly, good intentions often backfire. Slow and steady truly wins this race.

- **Stop moving at ninety miles an hour.** I know you feel a sense of urgency, and you want to find a replacement relationship ASAP because you "wasted" years of your life with your ex. Hold back. When you move too quickly, good intentions often backfire. Slow and steady truly wins this race.

- **Is he a pain reliever?** A migraine, a sore back, and a toothache are all very painful, and when you have one, you'll reach for just about anything to make the pain go away. Similarly, you may think a rebound guy will take away your heartfelt hurt and anguish. And you dive in head first, only to realize, as soon as your pain dwindles, that you have no interest in him. He's history—except he really liked you. Now you feel guilty for dumping him.

- **Your savior appears.** You meet someone who's going through a tough divorce, lots of legal stuff, and is dealing with a miserable, mean ex (or so you're told). He is compassionate, sexy, interesting, and thinks you're beautiful. You go away together for the weekend and the sex is amazing. You are on cloud nine—and then he disappears for a week. But then a dozen roses appear at your office, and you are so relieved. You can't wait to read the card. When do you, it says, "I wish I'd met you six months from now. You're great, but I am just not ready for a relationship. Wishing you all the best." Your heart sinks and you go into a meltdown, reliving how you felt when your husband told you he wanted a divorce.

- **Watch out for the ex factor.** You think you're ready to have a relationship, only to find out that you're comparing her to your ex. You react to her in the same way you did to your ex—often with sarcasm and hostility. And you wonder why she disappeared and doesn't return your calls.

However, a rebound relationship can actually be (sort of) good for you, too, helping you bounce back from your loss, according to a 2015 article in the Journal of Social and Personal Relationships. The positive outcomes reported included increased self-confidence, feeling more desirable, and overall feelings of well-being. And let's face it: Loneliness sucks, feeling unattractive is awful, and having no weekend plans is just plain depressing!

What else can a rebound do for you? Three main things:

1. **Cleanse your palate**. Dating someone new after your breakup can be a prelude to your next relationship adventure. It gets you ready for what you really want. It also keeps you from obsessing about your ex, and that's a great thing.

2. **Offer companionship**. It feels good to be in the company of someone special. This makes you feel like you've still got it—that's a huge step in moving forward!

3. **Give you hope for the future**. A rebound relationship, no matter how short term, can remind you that a romantic future is a possibility.

REBOUND RULES

If you're thinking about dating again before you feel fully healed from your breakup, promise me you will follow these Rebound Rules. And always, always listen to your gut and proceed with caution.

1. **Be candid and authentic**. It's important to be honest with yourself and your rebound guy or gal. State clearly what you're looking for. A one-night stand? Someone to restore your faith in "mankind?" A no-strings-attached relationship? Simply a fun time? Whatever it is, it's essential to let the person know that you're newly single and aren't looking for anything long-term. It's the right thing to do for you both.

2. **Steer clear of the ex clone**. If your rebound reminds you of your ex, especially everything that caused you

DECLUTTER YOUR APPEARANCE!

Now it's time to look in the mirror. What can you do to look your best? (And I'm not talking about major plastic surgery!) Invest some time and effort in whatever will boost your self-confidence right now. It'll be fun! It sure was for Samantha, who confessed, "I could not believe how I let myself go. My hair, my clothes— everything about me screamed 'depressed, pathetic, needy!' I booked a makeover appointment at a trendy salon. I got my hair cut, colored, straightened, and styled. I even got hair extensions. I had my eyebrows waxed, and I got a spa manicure and pedicure. After a day of beauty, I felt rejuvenated. My old self was coming back. I actually smiled when I looked in the mirror. On my next trip I'm going to buy one or two outfits I know I look fabulous in. I have to invest in myself. Looking better on the outside made me feel so much better on the inside."

misery and heartache, run as fast as you can. Recreating your past is not a good thing.

3. **Heartbreak times two.** The fact is that a rebound can cause heartbreak. If you are unwilling to experience rejection so soon after your breakup, a rebound relationship is not for you.

4. **Have realistic expectations.** Most rebounds are transitional relationships and have time limits. You have to know from the get-go that a rebound will not make everything right again. But if you're aware of this and the relationship still makes you smile, gives you some relief, and helps you process your breakup, all's good.

Ultimately, navigating the risks and benefits of a rebound relationship is tricky at best. And the best way to avoid a damaging rebound relationship is to give your heart sufficient healing time. You will know you are ready to date if your urge to meet someone new is driven by *desire* and not by *fear* of being without a mate.

❾ Escape into Your Job

Have a job that gets you out of the house and requires you to be on top of your game? Consider yourself lucky. Being forced to be fully involved and highly focused will help immensely. So, do not fall down on the job. I know you're going through a difficult process: Ask for help if you need it. It's okay to tell your boss and/or coworkers you are going through a breakup—as long as you also tell them you are capable of doing your job and aren't looking for pity or an excuse to take time off.

MOMENTARY MINI BREAKDOWNS ARE OKAY

Not everyone has the luxury of taking a week off to mourn a breakup. Perhaps you have kids, a job, or other responsibilities that won't go away so you can nurse your broken heart. If so, please know that it is okay to schedule time off from life—even if you feel like you're healing well. Build "off" time into your week. It could be an hour a week, or fifteen minutes a day. This is your time to yell, scream, cry, rest, journal, pray, or do anything you want to do to express your feelings. If these feelings don't have a healthy outlet, they'll get bottled up, and that could result in an explosion at the wrong time or place.

If you work at home, you're more apt to feel isolated, which can be tough in the fallout of a breakup. For instance, Maryann was working out of her home as a graphic designer while she was going through her divorce. She wished she had a job that got her out of the house every day because being at home made her feel so depressed. I advised her to take herself out for breakfast; go for a walk when she felt the sadness coming on; and make sure she got out of the house at least once a day. Maryann started scheduling lunch dates with friends and colleagues into her workdays, and it was exactly what she needed. Work can also help you:

Feel protected. Work can be your safe haven, so this may be just the right time to throw yourself totally into your job. That way you won't be able to dwell on your nasty breakup. And what a relief that is! Since you're spending so much time at work, you are accomplishing more, and you're sure to get oodles of praise from supervisors and colleagues. Excelling at work is wonderful for your self-esteem and your ability to rely on yourself!

Be distracted (in a good way) and feel normal. For Roz, a client of mine, work gave her a reason to "look good" every day (since she had to meet with customers), which actually made her feel better.

> "
>
> **Success is sometimes the outcome of a whole string of failures**
>
> —VINCENT VAN GOGH

Since she had to be engaging, chatty, and upbeat, her workday was an incredible distraction. There were days when she would fall into bed at 6 p.m. because being "on" all day was exhausting, but it was a small price to pay for feeling "normal" during the workday.

Feel appreciated. Tamara, a client who'd gone through an ugly divorce, had a team of six under her, and her staff needed her guidance on a daily basis. It was the only place in her life in which she felt worthwhile and needed. Her staff had no idea how much they were making Tamara feel valued and needed until a year after her divorce.

❿ Give of Yourself to Someone Who Needs You

You're probably thinking, How in the world can someone as devastated as I am be charitable to someone else? Well, guess what? Giving to others is an amazing way to feel better about yourself. It enables you to feel connected to another person, and to take the focus off yourself and your problems.

Here's what I recommend:

- **Do something for someone else.** Perform a random act of kindness for someone who has shown compassion toward you during your breakup (treat your coworker to lunch; send flowers to the friend who didn't leave your side for the first weekend after your split; or clean the snow off your neighbor's car).

- **Volunteer** at a homeless shelter; at a five-mile walk to raise funds for Alzheimer's disease; or at a crisis hotline. Volunteering is so healing because it has the power to put your breakup and your (good) life in perspective.

- **Run errands** for an elderly neighbor. It'll only take an hour of your time, but it'll be a lifesaver for the lady next door who has trouble getting around, or the guy down the hall who's recently bereaved.

- **Teach someone** who can use your skills and expertise. Are you an English teacher? Tutor your friend's daughter, the one who's struggling with her homework. Are you fluent in Spanish? Offer free lessons to someone who wants to learn. Do you love to bake? Show a friend how to make the perfect sourdough.

- **Donate** your time (babysitting, dog-sitting, house-sitting) or food to a local food bank.

- **Open yourself** to a person who needs emotional support, such as a friend or family member. You understand what suffering feels like—and focusing on someone else will distract you from your own pain.

As Winston Churchill said, "We make a living by what we get. We make a life by what we give." So don't let your pain and sadness prevent you from being generous and charitable to others who need you.

ONE DAY AT A TIME

I don't want you to worry about getting through the rest of your life. For now, think about what you have to do to get through today. Tomorrow, think about what you need to do to help yourself move forward to the next day. When each day becomes easier—and it will—you can start planning for the week. When that becomes easier, you can plan for the month. At about the three-month mark, you will be ready to start "thinking" about the rest of your life.

In Conclusion

Let's conclude Step 1 by reflecting on your breakup. Look back at your strengths, accomplishments, and triumphs during this life-altering time. These are perfect reminders of how resourceful and resilient you are. And they signify that you've come such a long way already. YEAH!

Now, ask yourself the following questions. Please jot down your answers quickly. There's no need to write anything long or even to use complete sentences: just use words or phrases, if you like.

What have you learned about yourself since your breakup? Make sure to include your strengths and accomplishments.

_____

_____

_____

_____

_____

_____

What has been most helpful in getting through your breakup?

_____

_____

_____

_____

_____

What are your top three pieces of advice for your friend whose boyfriend, girlfriend, husband, wife, or partner has just left her?

_____

_____

_____

_____

If you find yourself slipping backward—and we all do—reread this section. You can also look back at the reflections you just recorded to remind yourself of your strengths and of the things that have been most helpful during your post-breakup experience.

Joy is what
happens to us
when we allow
ourselves to
recognize how
good things
really are.

—MARIANNE WILLIAMSON,
SPIRITUAL TEACHER AND
BESTSELLING AUTHOR

FIND JOY: Advice for Diving into the Dating Pool with Confidence and Optimism

It may have taken awhile, but all your hard work has paid off. Your heart is mended, and your sadness and tears are part of your past, not your present. You're ready, willing, and able to put yourself out in the dating world. It's a little scary, sure, but that's normal. Plus, feeling motivated and slightly nervous at the same time actually keeps you focused, present, and on your toes.

You're determined to do what it takes to date with self-confidence and joy, and I'm truly excited for you. Thinking about how happy you'll be with someone you love—and who loves you and treasures time with you in return—gives me the chills. (It should do the same for you!) You're off to a great start, and I'm so glad to be part of your new adventure.

Here are some principles to focus on while jumping back into the dating pool:

- **Look forward to every date.** Each one is full of new potential!

- **Have a great time meeting lots of new people.** Even people who aren't your type can be fascinating and inspiring.

- **Learn about yourself from each date.** What works for you and what doesn't? What are your boundaries, limits, and values?

- **Be prepared for some bumps in the road.** You probably won't like everyone you meet, and vice versa. Let it go: That's part of life.

- **Always believe you are worth it.** Don't give up—ever.

- **If your date isn't right for you, don't panic.** It will be over in an hour!

Repeat after Me: "It's Just a Date"

This should be your new mantra. Dating is about having fun and getting to know someone. That's it. Don't waste your time worrying and obsessing over what it might (or might not) be like. You might be interested; you might not. She might be interested; she might not. Life will go on either way. And, remember, you aren't going to connect with every person you go out with any more than you'll love every car you test drive or every new recipe you try. That's part of what makes life interesting, right?

Think of dating as an opportunity to practice a skill—meeting new people—just like playing tennis, public speaking, or playing the piano. Since your last date may have been a while ago, now is the time to stick your toe in the proverbial water and see how it feels. If you think of dating simply as practice, you'll enjoy the process: You won't be running a grueling marathon to find the partner of your dreams. What a relief!

All you have to do on date number one is get to know him or her a little, enjoy yourself, and stay in the moment. It's that simple. Do not project into the future—it will only make you feel anxious, which will prevent you from being the fabulous, confident person you are.

Of course, dating after a breakup brings up many issues and concerns. Who should—or shouldn't—you go out with? Overthinking it is counterproductive. Remember, it's just a date! You need to practice meeting new people and talking about yourself. Besides, you never know where a new contact may lead: a new friend, a professional connection, and introduction to the person who turns out to be the next love of your life.

In the aftermath of your breakup, you want to date a variety of people so you can approach each date with anticipation, knowing that an enjoyable evening is your main goal. The more you date, the easier it will be to approach dating as your new favorite hobby.

First dates are an opportunity to see whether there will be a second date. Don't worry if all the items on your list aren't checked off. It doesn't matter. The more you date, the more you'll know what's indispensable for you. So what if your date lives thirty-five miles away, is four years younger, and is allergic to kiwi? Once you meet, you may be dying to go on a second date.

So, are you ready to go on the ride of your life? Good! The rest of this step will show you how to enjoy dating, minus the stress and awkwardness.

Here are a few things to keep in mind as you get started:

- Happiness can be elusive after a breakup.
- Dating will bring joy into your life.
- Suspend your judgment about dating.
- Think of dating as a foreign language you are learning for the first time.
- Today is a dating milestone: You are letting go of your fears, anxieties, and mixed feelings about getting back out there.

Now, here's why my mantra, "It's just a date," is so crucial for the plan to succeed: It keeps your mindset fresh and lets you approach each date with a sense of adventure, mystery, fun, and optimism. This is your insurance policy: It's the best way to foster satisfying, relaxed, connected dates. Ditch those outdated, pessimistic beliefs about dating. They aren't doing you any good.

Let's practice. Repeat after me: "I promise to approach every date with a sense of adventure, mystery, fun, and optimism, no matter what. I promise not to jump ahead to picking out my wedding dress or a name for my first-born child, or decorating the master bathroom with his and hers sinks. Even if my date turns out to be a date from hell, I am so grateful that I discovered what I needed to know in one short date. How lucky I am!"

I do know that dating isn't always a piece of cake. It takes time, effort, self-confidence, and—yes—hard work. But you can do it because you're determined to find a person who's the perfect fit for you.

Seven Clues You're Ready to Date

When is the right time to start dating after a breakup or divorce? There's no exact science—but there are signs to suggest you're ready. How many resonate with you? The more, the better!

1. YOU'VE LET GO OF YOUR ANGER.

The bitter, vicious anger you felt has evaporated, and it no longer rules your life. These days, you know that the sweetest revenge is living a happy life.

2. YOU'RE NO LONGER CLUELESS ABOUT THE ROLE YOU PLAYED IN YOUR BREAKUP.

After a lot of soul searching, you have gained insight into what's important in making a relationship work. And the way in which you contributed to the end of the relationship is also crystal clear.

3. YOU ARE NO LONGER OBSESSED WITH YOUR EX.

Your ex is a distant memory. What he's doing or who she's with is immaterial to you. Your ex no longer controls your every waking minute. You feel indifferent.

4. YOU'RE PRETTY SURE THAT BEING SINGLE IS NOT A FATAL DISEASE.

In fact, you're enjoying it. You can spend time with yourself and like it, too. You can pick and choose what makes you happy, and you have found new freedom in being accountable only to yourself. You are a capable, competent woman who can thrive on her own.

5. THE PROSPECT OF MEETING SOMEONE PUTS A SMILE ON YOUR FACE.

You find yourself paying attention to the people you come into contact with, wondering if they might be single. When you least expect it, you catch yourself daydreaming about how nice it would be to go on a date and feel desirable.

6. YOU LIKE THE WAY YOU LOOK.

Feeling self-confident in the looks department is essential. This isn't to say you have to transform yourself into a supermodel. It's about feeling attractive and comfortable in your own skin, projecting self-assurance, and carrying yourself with poise and charm. Being approachable in this way sends the message that you're worth being with.

7. YOU'RE GOING WITH YOUR GUT, NOT THE CALENDAR.

To put it simply, you just feel ready. There is no explicit time frame that dictates how long you should wait to start dating after your divorce or breakup. For some people, it could be a month; for others, it could be a year. You are ready to date when you want to enhance your life, not just ease the pain of the breakup or fill the void it leaves behind.

Play the Numbers Game

Dating is about numbers. The more people you go out with, the greater the possibility you'll find someone who's right for you. That can make dating feel like a second job. But this approach offers serious payoffs:

- The more people you meet, the greater your chance of finding a date.

- The more people you date, the greater your chance of connecting with the right person.

- The more dates you have with one person, the greater the chance of it developing into a meaningful relationship.

- The more you date, the more self-knowledge you gain: You'll know exactly what you do and don't want.

- Each date brings you closer to your goal of a happy, fulfilling relationship.

For instance, after Morgan, a woman I interviewed, went through a difficult divorce, she went on ninety first dates in a year and a half. Yes, you heard me right. She saw each first date as an opportunity to meet someone whom she might want to see again and who "had potential" in her eyes. Morgan's resilience, perseverance, and, most importantly, her positive spin on the dating process had a happy ending: She met the man of her dreams and is now happily married.

Then there's Gabby, a former client of mine, who told me she was no good at dating. But more than anything, she wanted to meet a woman with whom she could have a fulfilling relationship. Gabby said that she limited herself to going out on two dates per month. After three months and no second dates, I suggested that Gabby bump up her numbers. She finally agreed to go on eight first dates during the next two months. And she reported back to me that she finally got it. "The more dates I go on, the easier the whole dating thing is, and I even had several second dates," she told me. "I had no idea it could be fun, and it is!"

Choose a Dating Coach

Remember your breakup pals? They were there for you when you were a total mess in the first weeks after your breakup. Now it's time to "hire" a dating coach to be there for you during this (much more enjoyable) process. Your dating coach can be your best friend, your cousin, a paid dating coach, or another single friend who needs a coach as well.

But wait–why do you need a coach? Basically, you need to be accountable to someone else. Your dating coach is your cheerleader, someone who'll keep you focused, driven, and won't let you give up when the going gets tough.

What does a good dating coach look like?

IF YOUR DATING COACH IS ALSO YOUR FRIEND, HERE ARE SOME FUN THINGS TO DO TOGETHER:

- Go clothes shopping and be each other's stylist. It'll give you a major confidence boost!

- Go out to lunch, to a museum, the gym, a mall, a party, or a football game. Once you're there, you and your dating coach are to approach people you don't know and start conversations with them. It doesn't matter if they are women or men, older or younger. This is just practice! It's easier to approach someone you don't know if you have a friend with you.

- Attend a singles' event. Ask your coach to be your wingman: Have him introduce you to someone you'd like to meet. The best wingwoman is your partner in crime, your accomplice, your confidante. She doesn't take herself too seriously; has a great sense of humor; and gets you meeting, mingling, and talking. And the more playful the two of you are together, the better the results!

She or he is:

- **Someone who adores you.** You want a coach who wants you to be happy and wants you to meet a great partner.

- **Male or female; single or married; gay or straight.** Whoever your dating coach is, she or he will offer a unique perspective.

- **Understanding.** Your coach gets it: Dating is complicated and emotional.

- **Caring.** Your coach will be there for you when you're feeling down and disenchanted.

- **Goal-directed.** Your coach keeps you moving.

- **Upbeat.** She or he has a great sense of humor.

- **Positive.** Your coach has to keep you hopeful and encourage you to believe that dating will lead to a loving relationship and partnership.

Your coach will also help you set goals to increase the number of people you meet and to move your dating plan forward. Write out your plan and give a copy to your dating coach, then check in with that person once a week to report how you are doing and to get feedback. Your plan should have goals that are attainable and measurable. You'll learn exactly how to do this in Step 5 (see page 137), but the following five check marks are a sample monthly plan that will get you thinking and provide you with structure and direction:

✔ Tell three to five people you know that you are back on the dating market.

✔ Respond to two or three online dating profiles each week.

✔ Ask one or two online matches out for coffee or a drink.

✔ Attend one or two singles' events.

✔ Organize a happy hour and ask everyone to bring a single friend.

Talk to your dating coach about what you are doing to meet new people, how your dates are going, and how you're feeling about your new dating life. Share your concerns and worries, too. Let your coach know you're open to constructive criticism and would like to hear both positive and negative feedback. If a date goes well and you don't hear back from your date afterward, ask your coach how to proceed. Or if you get dating jitters, ask your coach to talk you through them.

If your coach is too easy on you, and you don't feel you're getting the push you need, ask him to take it to the next level: You can handle it!

How to Find a Dating Coach for Hire

You can also hire a professional dating coach to support you as you re-enter the world of dating. Here's how to find one:

- Ask friends for recommendations. Word of mouth is often the best source.
- Look online. Do an Internet search for "dating coach" or "dating help." There are lots of coaches who offer phone, Skype, online, and in-person coaching.
- Check out online dating sites that have articles written by dating coaches whom you might be able to contact.

WHAT SHOULD YOU LOOK FOR IN A PAID DATING COACH?

He or she should be someone who:

- Makes you feel comfortable and at ease
- Helps you identify your blind spots and what's preventing you from finding love
- Is goal oriented and offers practical suggestions and tips
- Is honest and direct
- Works collaboratively with you so you feel like you're both on the same team
- Explains the services offered and their cost
- Follows through on what she says she will provide

As a dating coach, I'm explicit about the dating realities that everyone knows deep down but needs to hear spoken aloud. A dating coach might not always tell you what you want to hear, but honesty really is the best policy. Here are some truths that a professional dating coach should bring up with you:

- You can't wish away dating anxiety and nervousness, but you can minimize and, ultimately, master it.
- You won't attract every guy or be attracted to every woman. That's fine: All you need is a relationship in which there's a mutual attraction.
- Not everyone will like you or want to date you–that's okay.
- Dating is not an exact science. You measure your success by your own yardstick.
- There is no crystal ball that'll tell you exactly where you'll meet Mr. or Ms. Dream Come True, so always be on the love patrol lookout!

Getting Feedback from a Paid Dating Coach

Feedback from a dating coach helps you be proactive about dating; enhances your self-awareness; raises your self-confidence; and gives you the tools to be the best dater you can be so you can realize your goal of finding love. Here's an example from my own practice: Nicole was divorced after a fifteen-year marriage and hadn't dated since college. For Nicole, coming home to an empty apartment

YOUR SINGLE FRIENDS ARE YOUR BEST ALLIES

Apart from your dating coach, it's time to dig up your single friends or to make new ones. Dating can be a roller coaster, and it's important to be able to share your experiences with single friends. After all, they get it! Plus, going out for a fun evening with your new single buddies is a great confidence boost. And it's comforting to connect with other singles who are happier now than when they were in miserable relationships. You can be a great source of support for your single friends, too. Helping someone else is an amazing way to feel good, and the advice you're dishing out helps everyone.

was hard, but the weekends were the toughest. She came to see me because she needed help getting her dating life back on track. We role played and simulated initial phone calls and first dates, discussed ways to tell a date that she had a great time, and what to say when she wasn't interested.

I offered suggestions for making her online dating profile more engaging and how to rule in possible matches rather than rule them out (we increased the radius of where her dates lived from ten to twenty-five miles). After each date, Nicole would report back to me on how the date went, and I would offer tips. For instance, I suggested that she ask her date more questions to demonstrate interest and to display welcoming, approachable body

language (her body language tended to be stiff and distant). I even took photos during our session to show her what her body language looked like. We took "before" and "after" photos: Nicole had no idea she was presenting herself as aloof, stiff, and disinterested until she saw herself in the photos.

Date coaching is to romance as personal training is to fitness. Both coaches set goals, map out a plan, offer feedback, and motivate clients to break out of their comfort zones so they can reach their goals.

The Golden Rules of Dating

Remember, you reap what you sow. It's important to treat others the same way you want to be treated. Most of these "rules" are actually just common sense, but they're worth reviewing before you embark on your dating journey.

1. **Be nice.** Be generous with compliments; keep criticisms to yourself; be kind. This isn't just courteous; it'll also build your confidence and reduce the dating jitters we all have.

2. **Don't forget to say thank you.** Thank her if she picks up the tab, or if he holds the door for you. And thank her at the end of the date if you had a good time. Your date will take notice of your graciousness.

3. **Always tell the truth.** If you want to see him again, let him know; if you don't, gently tell him you don't feel a connection and wish him the best. Although it may hurt in the moment, it's the best gift you can give someone. If total honesty seems too awkward, say, "It was nice to meet you; I wish you good fortune in your search." That makes it pretty clear that you aren't interested. Or, this one will catch him off guard: Tell him if he's interested, you have a friend that you think would be perfect for him. If he says yes, tell him you'll ask your friend if she's up for it and will get back to him. In any case, though, if you're sure you aren't interested, let him know. You know how it feels when you aren't sure whether someone wants to see you again and how helpful it is to know the truth.

4. **Be the type of person you want to date.** If you want someone who is kind, secure, energetic, thoughtful, hard-working, fun, and loving, then be that person. You will attract what you project.

5. **Date fairly.** Balance the date by talking about yourself, asking questions, listening, and showing interest in what your date says; this will make her (and you) feel comfortable.

The Dating Rules That Are Meant to Be Broken

The Golden Rules of Dating are the only rules you need to follow. The rules below, on the other hand, are not your friends. They limit your chances of finding love because they impose artificial restrictions and prevent you from being spontaneous, making new connections, and having new experiences. These roadblocks will stop you from finding the love you deserve.

✘ Always wait twenty-four hours before you text your date.

✔ Let your date know if you had a good time.

There is no logical reason to wait twenty-four hours if you want to text your date and say that you had an awesome time. It's fine to send a short text that says any of the following:

"It was so great to meet you."

"I had so much fun."

"I would love to get together again."

Your date will be delighted to know you had a great time and are interested in date number two. This will encourage him to contact you right away because he knows you are receptive.

Don't kick yourself, though, if you don't hear back: Instead, praise yourself for letting him know that you liked him. You can move on knowing you were confident enough to express how you felt.

✘ Never accept a last-minute date.

✔ Be spontaneous once in a while.

It's okay to accept a spur-of-the-moment date. I know what you're wondering: Will that make you look too available or maybe even desperate? No, no, no! It says you're not booked for that date and time, and that you're okay with being sponta-neous. And last-minute dates are often the best ones, because you don't have time to overthink it. (One caveat, though: This last-minute stuff shouldn't become the norm. This is fine for a first date, and for occasional spontaneity, but it shouldn't take the place of "planned" dates.)

✘ Only date one person at a time.

✔ Play the field to learn what you like and don't like.

There's no reason to take yourself off the market unless you and your date have decided to be exclusive. Dating more than one person at a time can be a good thing: You're casting a wide net and taking time to figure out who's the right fit for you. That said, I'm not suggesting you become a serial dater and date just for the sake of dating. That's counterproductive to finding a relationship.

✖ **Wait two days to return a phone call.**

✔ **Respond to a phone call within twenty-four hours.**

You always thought it was good to play hard to get because all guys love the chase. Not so. Guys find it irresistible when you show a genuine desire to go out with them.

Playing hard to get can cause your date to lose interest and move on—all while you're still playing the telephone waiting game.

✖ **The only "real" dates take place on Saturday nights.**

✔ **A good date can happen any day of the week.**

Don't fall into a self-imposed trap over when a date "should" occur. "Real" dates can take place any day (or night) of the week: This does not dictate the value of the date. After all, everyone has different working hours, days off, or prior commitments. Do not measure your value by the day of the week on which your date occurs.

✖ **Never ask a guy out.**

✔ **Definitely ask a guy out!**

If you're a heterosexual woman, you're probably used to letting guys do the hard work. It's time to break out of your comfort zone and try something wild and crazy. It's good to take advantage of opportunities that might not present themselves again. You have to act quickly! Here are some examples:

It could be the guy sitting next to you on the train whom you just had a fabulous conversation with; or it could be the bank teller who's always so happy to see you and eager to chat and who tells you that today is his last day of work; or it could be the guy at the gym with whom you had an instant connection but who told you that his membership was about to expire. If you don't make a move now, he will vanish, and you won't have a second chance. I know it's awkward, and that you wish he'd make the first move. But we never know how anyone else feels until we take a walk in his shoes. So, here's your chance to try on his shoes!

So, what's the worst that can happen when you ask a guy out?

- He might give you the brush off.
- He might respond with a one-or two-word answer.
- He quickly says he has to get going.
- He tells you he is married or in a relationship.
- He simply says no.

None of these will put a smile on your face, right? Wrong! They should—because you took a (huge!) chance and decided to go for it, no matter what the outcome. Plus, the more often you approach a guy, the more comfortable and natural it becomes. And, finally, being turned down by some people leaves room to be accepted by others.

What's the best that can happen when you ask a guy out?

- He's thrilled you approached him.
- He wants to continue the conversation.

- He asks for your phone number.
- You have a nice conversation that doesn't go any further.
- He tells you that he's wanted to talk to you for a while and is so glad you made the first move.

All of these positive responses will make you smile from ear to ear for sure! And here's what I want you to remember: You never know when your approach will lead to a date. The more approaching you do, the more fun you'll have, and the greater the chances that you'll get to a yes. You gotta be in it to win it!

Still, I know asking a guy out on a date is daunting. So here are a few suggestions, complete with risk levels: high risk (HR); medium risk (MR); low risk (LR). Mix and match according to your personal style and the situation in which you find yourself.

High Risk

"I have to confess, I hoped that you would ask me out—so instead of waiting, I'm asking you out. Would you like to grab a pizza and beer?"

"I've never asked a guy out before—you are my first! Would you like to go out on Friday night?"

Medium Risk

"I really enjoyed talking with you. Would you like to go out sometime?"

"We seem to have so much to talk about. How about meeting for a drink after work sometime?"

Low Risk

"You know that new Mexican place that just opened? How about checking it out? Let's exchange numbers so we can make a plan to get together."

"I'm in the mood for a latte. Would you like to join me?"

"Would you like to continue this conversation over a cup of coffee?"

"Here's my card. It would be great to see you again."

Overcome Your Fear

First of all, fearless first dates do not exist. Anyone who says otherwise is just masking their nervousness and trying to fake it! And fear isn't necessarily a bad thing: A little fear is fabulous, but a lot of fear is debilitating. Fear requires energy; and since you won't be able to make it disappear (though that would be nice!) you must face your fears and use them to move forward instead of letting them hold you back.

Dating can make you feel as though you're in front of a magnifying mirror. You imagine that your shortcomings and flaws will be uncovered, and you approach your first date with feelings of uncertainty and vulnerability.

Many women who have gone through a breakup have avoided dating for a year or two. They stop themselves from getting back out there by making excuses to themselves:

"I'm not 100 percent ready."

"I'm so out of practice."

"I wouldn't even know where to start."

"It's just too much work."

The bottom line is that they—like you—don't want another failed relationship, and being vulnerable is hard after a breakup.

I'm a worrier by nature, too. So let's get all our fears out in the open and figure out what to do about them. Ready? Of course you are, because worrying and fear just plain suck.

Reframe Rejection

The number one roadblock to getting back into the dating world is the fear of rejection. Even thinking about being rejected has made many of my clients reluctant to put themselves back on the market. Their logic is, If I don't date, then I can't be rejected, and after what I've been through, I can't bear the thought of any more rejection. Then come the what-if's: What if he doesn't call? What if it ends after four dates? What if I don't get a second date?

Reframing rejection gives you the ability to see rejection as a gift—something to be thankful for. Tell yourself this:

"My date has just done me the biggest favor. She let me know very quickly that we are not right for each other. Because she let me know right away, I am closer to finding the relationship that's a good fit for me. I only invested a single date—not a month, a year, or a decade. I want to thank her for not wasting my time."

Dump that Fear of Abandonment

Think of your first date as an opportunity to sample a variety of guys. Don't waste your time obsessing and worrying about what will happen if you get into a relationship and he wants to end it. Remember your mantra: It's just a date! When your fear of being left alone creeps up on you, focus on the next date, and nothing else. After all, by the middle of your date, you might find yourself wishing your friend would text you with a "hair emergency" to get you out of there fast!

Control Your Catastrophic Thinking

Catastrophic thinking is imagining the worst possible outcome of a situation. Your anxiety will fuel the fire and your mind will focus on every conceivable negative consequence. For instance, imagine you're on your way to meet your date and you get lost. You know you'll be late. You can go into panic mode and convince yourself that she will bail; you can go straight home because you know she will think you're an idiot; you can text your date and tell her you were captured by aliens or that your GPS started speaking in a foreign language; or, you can take a deep breath, call or text your date, and simply tell her that you got lost and will be there in ten minutes. It's your choice.

Abandon Your Fear of Embarrassment

I know you're flooded with what-ifs right now. What if I say something stupid? What if I have a sneezing fit? What if I don't like the food I ordered? What if I forget his name? Well, the best antidote to doing something embarrassing is to make light of it, laugh about it, or show your vulnerability and have the guts to say:

"This is *so* embarrassing." (as you smile and shake your head)

"Is my face turning beet red?" (as you touch your cheeks)

"Next it's your turn to do something embarrassing so we can be even." (as you chuckle at yourself)

"I promised myself I wouldn't do anything to embarrass myself; I guess I can't take my own advice!" (Smile and laugh as you say this one!)

Any of these lines will take the edge off an awkward situation, and turn it into something to laugh about later. And the funny (and reassuring) thing about dating anxiety is that everyone has it: They just manifest it in different ways. If you find yourself feeling nervous during your first date, you can say, "Do you ever get nervous on first dates? Because I do." Your date may be so nervous herself that she'll be eternally grateful to you for bringing it up. Once your nervousness is out in the open, guess what? The anxiety disappears.

Triumph over Your Fear of Intimacy and Commitment

It's your first date, but you find yourself thinking, "I can't imagine having sex with someone new," or "I have to keep my guard up," or "What if he wants a commitment before I'm ready?" All of these fears are natural after a breakup or divorce. Focus on staying in the present and accept what's happening in the here and now without judgment. Concentrate on getting to know your date and imagine what a second date would be like (or not)!

It's okay to be scared as long as you're simultaneously brave. Besides, once you finally go on that very first date after your breakup, your fears will dissipate because you're doing what scares you. Often the anticipatory anxiety is a hundred times worse than whatever it is you're scared of.

Re-Examine Your Dating Don'ts

Are you unwittingly limiting your dating opportunities because of arbitrary "standards" you've set? These standards will do nothing except prevent you from meeting great people.

Here are the most popular dating don'ts:

✖ Don't date a person with children.
✖ Don't date a person who has been divorced more than once.
✖ Don't date someone who is younger than you.
✖ Don't date someone who is shorter than you.
✖ Don't date a person who earns less money than you do.
✖ Don't date a person who isn't your "type."
✖ Don't date a coworker.
✖ Don't have a long-distance relationship.
✖ Don't date someone you meet in a bar.
✖ Don't date someone who is retired.
✖ Don't date someone bald.

Why would you limit yourself this way? I'm not suggesting that you lower your standards, settle, or date for the sake of dating. I'm urging you not to cross a great person off your list just because he lives some distance away or is an inch shorter than you. These factors have little or no effect on the ultimate success of a relationship.

It's also a good to time to be honest about your deal breakers. Maybe you are 100 percent sure you want to have kids. Don't waste your time dating people who make it 100 percent clear they don't. Evaluate your list of must-haves and be sure they are the true essentials. If they are flexible, allow that to widen the number of people you consider dating.

Turn Dating Into Your New Hobby

You have made it past the first major hurdle and you've successfully gone on at least one first date! Congrats–that's a big deal! Now instead of thinking of dates as a "once in a while" event, think about how you can make dating part of your regular routine. Here are some helpful guidelines.

Make Time

You have to carve out time in your busy life for dating. Everything else will get in the way unless you make it a priority. After all, your date needs to feel that you want to spend time with her and that you have time in your life for a relationship. It's a delicate balance: No one likes to feel as if he is just another entry on your to-do list. At the same time, it's not all or nothing. Enthusiasm is great, but finding a balance with your other interests will make dating much more satisfying. Don't give up volunteering, and don't ditch your exercise class or book club. Make time for dating, but stay connected to other parts of your life.

The Rule of Three

This one is important. If you like him but still feel some ambivalence, I suggest that you go out on three dates. Here's why: On date number one, you're both a bit nervous and sizing each other up. On date number two, you're a little more at ease; and by date number three, your confidence has peaked, and you will know

whether or not you want to proceed. By going on three dates, you have the opportunity to see the person in a variety of circumstances.

The Ex Factor

Never take your ex with you on dates. She's history, and you shouldn't let her take up time when your mission is to make a fabulous first impression. I know it's tempting to spill your guts about your divorce or breakup, but the gory details belong in your therapist's office, not on a date. Make a pact with yourself that you will not allow memories of your ex to ruin your date. Since your aim is to get better at your new hobby (dating), don't wreck it with negativity and hurt from your past. Remember, hobbies are fun, pleasurable activities that bring you joy. So, when asked why you broke up or got divorced, reach for one of the answers on the right– you'll steer the conversation away from that topic in seconds.

You don't want to scare off a really good date with ex bashing. That's the perfect way to sabotage your chance of connecting.

The same goes for him, too. If you find yourself on the receiving end of an ex-bashing rant, you might feel like responding with an angry story of your own–don't take the bait. Change the subject, finish your drink, and call it a night. On the other hand, if he's too close to his ex, that isn't a good sign, either: If he lets you know right from the start that she is his confidante and that they have dinner together every week because she's such a great cook, be wary. Being civil with your ex is great, but confiding in her, going to weddings and events with her, and dining regularly with her? I don't think so.

Find the Perfect One

Think it's impossible? Nope. It boils down to valuing the fifty things about that person that are "perfect" and accepting the ten things that are "imperfect." All relationships have minor imperfections, and searching for "the one who's flawless in every way" is a waste of time, because he doesn't exist. When you feel appreciated and loved, overlooking the small stuff is no biggie. Keep your goal in mind: Your aim is to have fun, meet new prospects, and discover more and more about what you want in your next relationship.

Spot Mr. Wrong (Then Get Out of There)

In the early stages of a relationship, how you are treated is the best indicator of how you will be treated in the future. If you start getting signals that things are doomed, trust yourself—once you chuck Mr. Wrong, you'll be able to find Mr. Right.

HOW YOU FEEL WHEN YOU'RE WITH HIM

You're walking on eggshells. Do you analyze your actions and words out of fear your date will get angry or put you down? Walking on eggshells will not prevent Mr. Wrong from getting upset. It's draining, and it'll destroy your self-esteem.

You get a knot in your stomach—and not in a good way. His name pops up on your phone or you see an email from him with a vague subject line and your stomach drops: Is he cancelling again? Constant anxiety is not part of a healthy relationship.

You're doing all the work. Do you put in tons of effort to make your date happy? This is not sustainable. Cut your losses and head for the door.

AVOIDING EX TALK

"I'd much rather get to know you than talk about how my marriage fell apart."

"The relationship was broken: We tried to repair it, but ultimately we decided to split."

"In a nutshell, my husband said he was done and wanted out. He does not deserve any air time here: I'd much rather get to know you."

"How about we hold off on the exes until we get to know each other better?"

"It was complicated, and I don't want to ruin our night talking about my ex."

HOW HE ACTS AROUND YOU

Critical of your appearance—especially things you can't change. Does he constantly criticize your facial features, body, or weight? There is no place in a healthy relationship for talk that is disrespectful or humiliating.

He never believes you. You tell your date you had dinner with friends. He says, "Yeah, right." You laugh it off, but he demands what he thinks is the truth. Get rid of him now.

He's the ultimate "mansplainer." No matter what, he knows better. If he never utters "maybe you're right," move on.

He lies or exaggerates the truth. Your date says he is the vice president of his company, but you discover that he's a part-time salesman. If you can't be sure he's honest, you'll always doubt him, even when he tells the truth.

He never calls when he says he will. If he's into you, he'll call when he says he will—and when you least expect it, because you're always on his mind.

He promises the world but delivers nothing. If he breaks promises, don't ignore it. Mr. Can't-Count-On-Me *has* a choice—he'll make it loud and clear.

He doesn't introduce you to his friends or family. If your date is genuinely interested in you, he'll want everyone to meet you. No introductions once your relationship is exclusive? Ask why.

Commitment is not in his vocabulary. You tell your date you've never been happier—then he stops calling, says he wants to slow down. Things get better, but he says he feels pressured. If you're looking for something long-term, it won't be with this guy.

Think of these red flags as flashing lights that signal danger. And remember— Mr. Wrong is just a bump in the road!

IT'S OKAY TO SAY NO TO DATES.

You heard me right! Just because someone asks doesn't mean you have to say yes. In fact, you *should* turn down a date if he comes across as creepy, strange, taken, or if you simply know in your gut that the situation doesn't feel right. Sometimes it's best not to overanalyze. You are in charge of your dating life, and if a potential date doesn't feel right to you, it's not. Trust yourself.

Who Pays on a First Date?

Although gender roles are no longer as clearly defined as they once were, one old-fashioned dating custom still rings true with money.

In my experience, the majority of women want men to pay on the first date. It sets a romantic vibe and is a concrete way for him to show he's interested and able to "provide" for you. Still, if you are a woman who always wants the guy to pay for the first date, be considerate of the cost. Let's face it: First dates can get expensive. And the bottom line is that it's inappropriate to expect a stranger to foot the bill for an over-the-top restaurant on a first date.

If a guy suggests an expensive place, say, "Let's hold off going to such a nice place for now. How about in a couple of weeks instead?" Suggest a burger joint, a pizza place, a cup of coffee, a walk, the mall food court, or a cozy bar for one drink. If you're on a coffee date that's going well and he asks you to dinner afterward, suggest a place that's reasonably priced so he won't feel pressured to pick a high-priced spot. This way he knows you don't need, want, or expect to be wined and dined. A guy who wants to spend a lot on date number one is misguided in his judgment. He might hope that taking you to a place you love will get you to like him—which we all know never works. And it's also important for you not to see first dates as a meal ticket.

When a woman offers to pay the tab, most men immediately think she has no interest in him. So when he offers to pick up the tab, smile and say, "Thanks so much." If that doesn't feel right for you, or if you want to be more specific, say:

"Next time drinks are on me."

"If you're in the mood for dessert, I know a yummy place and it's my treat."

"I'd be happy to split the bill, if you'd like."

"Thanks for dinner. Next time I'll pay."

"Dating can be expensive; don't you think? Since we had a great time, let's toss a coin—winner pays!"

"Could I leave the tip?"

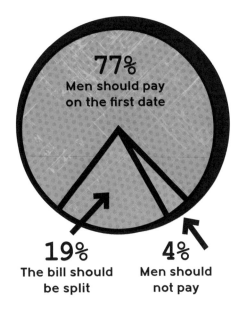

77% Men should pay on the first date

19% The bill should be split

4% Men should not pay

» The results of a 2014 Nerd Wallet Survey, which asked 1,000 men and women in relationships: "Do you think men should pay for the first date?"

Beyond Dinner and a Movie
Fun Activities to Do Together

It's time to get out there and date! Don't want to stick to the traditional dinner-and-a-movie script? Never fear: I've prepared a list of great date activities with more than just the ordinary options. When you're selecting an activity, think about what might be fun, encourage conversation, or set a romantic tone. This doesn't have to be expensive, either; money is not the best indicator of a date's success. The truth is that your date can cost next to nothing and still be sensational!

What makes a great date?

- Helps you get to know each other.
- Brings you closer together.
- Involves a shared activity.
- Demonstrates that you have taken time to plan something special.

Inspiring, out-of-the-ordinary activities

- Garage sale
- Palm reading
- Zoo
- Amusement park
- Drive-in movie
- Scary movie
- Local theater production
- Check the newspaper for interesting and unusual events in your area
- Sporting event
- Hot-air balloon ride
- Rent a fancy car for a few hours
- Classic car show
- Ride in a horse-drawn carriage
- Street fair
- Hit the casino (set a manageable budget you can afford to lose)
- Five-star brunch
- Take a CPR class

Ideas for foodies

- A dinner cruise
- A tour of a local winery, brewery, or chocolate factory
- Cook together
- Seek out unique restaurants, try a tasting menu; order fondue; go to a vegetarian Indian buffet; sample a cuisine you've never had before, like Turkish, Cuban, or sushi

Active dates

- Exercise together (run a 5k, take a yoga class, go for a jog, play golf or tennis)
- Ride a bike built for two
- Bowling
- Mini golf
- Try something extreme such as sky diving, whitewater rafting, kayaking, or rock climbing
- Ice skating

Date-friendly freebies (Good dates don't have to be expensive!)

- Watch a sunrise
- See some fireworks
- Walk on the beach
- Volunteer together
- Build a snowman or make a sandcastle

- Go to a museum (visit www.museumfreedays. com for local free admission days)
- Attend an outdoor concert

- Have a free lunch (find free food samples at the grocery store or food market)
- Check out your library for free classes, book signings, and movie nights

My top picks

- Plan a mystery date.
- Be a tourist in your own town.
- Take a day trip.
- Have a "progressive" dining experience–appetizers at one restaurant, main courses at another, and dessert at a third.

Be Your Own Dating Service

It's time to let out the secret! Say it loud and clear: You're back on the dating market. Let everyone know that you welcome the opportunity to be "fixed up." And be sure to take the pressure off your matchmakers by telling them they're not responsible for finding you the perfect date or mate. You're ready to date again and could use their help when it comes to giving your phone number to potential dates. They'll be excited and happy to help: Everyone loves to play matchmaker. Try being a matchmaker for someone else and see how it feels: Your single friends will love you for it.

Here's another approach if you're willing to be outrageous. Tell your matchmaker that you are offering dinner at the most exclusive restaurant, the hottest show tickets in town, or a weekend getaway at a fabulous spa if she introduces you to the love of your life. "Really?!" Your matchmaker will wonder . . .

"Yes," you'll say. "Absolutely. I'm counting on you because I know you have great taste, and it's a small price to pay for finding love again, so thanks for keeping me in mind!" Your friend will love the challenge, and, with that kind of incentive, she's sure to keep you in mind the next time she meets anyone eligible.

So don't get fixated on finding someone who's your "type." Concentrate instead on finding someone who is totally and completely in love with who you are—even your quirks and flaws. You might discover that the mate of your dreams is nothing like anyone you've ever dated.

WHAT'S MY TYPE?

Did your ex meet all your "qualifications?" On paper, he may have had everything you thought was important, including money, looks, prestige, and a similar background. Even his car was appealing. You thought you'd finally scored a home run—except that you never felt safe, appreciated, important, or desired.

Create a Dating Uniform

For me, the most nerve-wracking, time-consuming part of dating–the part I detested most–was getting ready. I'd try on a million outfits before I went back to the very first one I tried. My bedroom was a total mess, and things would quickly escalate to a state of panic because I couldn't find my favorite earrings or the perfect necklace.

Finally, I decided that the only remedy for this was to create a "dating uniform." Seriously. I picked out a few outfits that were super flattering and that I felt great in. Then I chose one of these for each date. It was such a relief to feel organized as I prepared for my date. I had no more pre-date meltdowns, which meant I was calm and relaxed before heading out the door–and there was no mess to clean up when I got home. Choosing a dating uniform was a win-win for me. Feeling comfortable and confident ensures you will come across as self-assured, not self-conscious.

Tips for choosing your uniform include:

- **Wear what you love and feel attractive in.** If you have a favorite top, buy it in multiple colors. When you feel appealing, you'll act that way.

- **Make sure it flatters you.** You might love super-tight jeans or short skirts–but are they the styles that look best on you? Don't wear something just because it's in or because your best friend looks great in it.

- **Don't worry about repeating your outfit.** This is a first date, remember? So you can safely wear it over and over.

- **Comfort and fit are indispensable.** The last thing you want to be doing is tucking in your shirt all night, or yanking your skirt down, or pulling up your jeans every time you sit down.

Now you've got the skills, confidence, and knowledge you need to make joyful dating your new favorite pastime, so it's time to show off those admirable assets.

If you don't go after what you want, you'll never have it. If you don't ask, the answer is always no. If you don't step forward, you're always in the same place

-NORA ROBERTS,
ROMANCE NOVELIST

Step 3

FLAUNT IT: Become a Fabulous Flirt

You've embraced dating with joy and enthusiasm, and you're so ready to get back into the dating groove. But what if you feel like your flirting skills are more than a little rusty? Well, this step will show you how to become a practiced-yet-effortless equal-opportunity flirt. Soon, you'll see opportunities everywhere. The hot guy in front of you in line at the bank? The cute gas station attendant who flags you down so he can wash your car windows? The adorable woman you just made eye contact with at the bar? You'll be able to strike up a conversation with anyone with plenty of confidence and charm. The same goes for the digital dating world, too.

It's entirely natural to feel hesitant and awkward about flirting. Not to worry, you'll get your flirt back better than ever. I've reawakened dormant "flirting DNA" in hundreds of women. Having followed my advice, they have transformed the way in which they view flirting and the benefits it offers.

It doesn't matter how long it's been since you approached a guy or signaled your interest in him. You can still do this! Now is the time to test the romantic waters, to learn to reveal your attraction in small doses. Flirting is like fishing: You bait your line and cast it out again and again—and when you least expect it, you reel in a great catch.

First, let's see how your flirting knowledge stacks up. Take the little quiz below to find out.

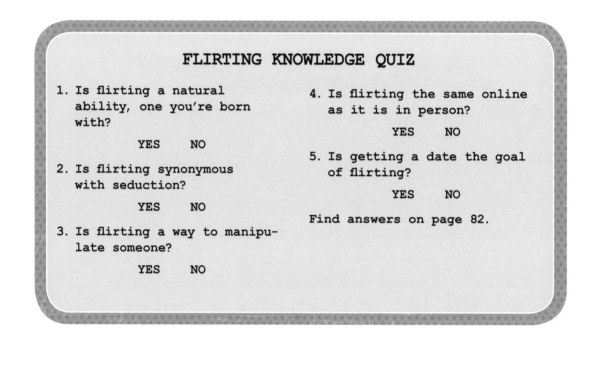

FLIRTING KNOWLEDGE QUIZ

1. Is flirting a natural ability, one you're born with?

      YES   NO

2. Is flirting synonymous with seduction?

      YES   NO

3. Is flirting a way to manipulate someone?

      YES   NO

4. Is flirting the same online as it is in person?

      YES   NO

5. Is getting a date the goal of flirting?

      YES   NO

Find answers on page 82.

Flirting is fun but often misunderstood. It allows you to meet someone you'd ordinarily be reluctant or scared to approach. Your flirtatious encounter could lead to a date, a friendship, a relationship, a marriage, a fabulous evening, a professional connection, or it might simply be a terrific experience that'll stay with you for a lifetime. When you flirt with someone, a kind of magic happens: It's exhilarating for the flirter and is an amazing ego boost for the flirtee. And the more you flirt, the more energized and joyful you will feel.

And sometimes flirting can happen in the most fun, natural way.

For instance, Daniella and her boyfriend of two years broke up three months ago. Tonight is the first night she's officially back in circulation. She has her dry-clean-only jeans on, plus her favorite pair of heels. She has blown out and re-blown out her hair so it's the perfect combination of messy and straight.

Daniella arrives at the party and the first person she sees is the guy she was hoping would be there: her friend Stacy's cousin, Zack. Stacy has raved about him, and there he is, right in front of her. What does Daniella do? She becomes paralyzed with nerves and makes a dash for the ladies' room. On her way out of the bathroom, she quickly returns to where Zack is standing. He is holding a drink and has a huge grin on his face as Daniella walks by. Daniella thinks this is his way of saying hi, so she introduces herself. He keeps smiling. Then he taps her on the shoulder

THE BEST WAY TO GET A DATE? STAY IN THE MOMENT

Your chances of getting a phone number or a date will increase if you take the focus off doing so: Instead, stay in the moment; go with the flow. This way, you focus on the connection you're making in the moment, not on future expectations. Being spontaneous is the best way to make a connection with someone.

and points to her shoe. You guessed right: Daniella was dragging about a foot of toilet paper behind her. They had a good laugh about it, and it was the perfect flirting icebreaker. They exchanged numbers, and in the months to come, they told their toilet paper story to their friends about a gazillion times.

See, that doesn't sound too scary, does it? That's because it's not! In fact, now is a good time to define our terms. Let's talk about what flirting is and isn't.

Flirting Demystified

Flirting is an intricate dance combining inviting body language and captivating words. The best flirting is done with humor, playfulness, and a relaxed, upbeat state of mind. It can consist of an appealing smile, a longing glance, a wink, a gentle touch, or even a sizzling handshake. Listen: If Antony and Cleopatra knew how to do it, you can learn, too. (These days you even have technology to help you!)

So what, exactly, is flirting?

• Flirting is the best icebreaker and tension reducer. It allows you to be light-hearted, a bit mischievous, and super casual without the "ooh, baby baby" come-on seriousness of seduction. Skillful flirts know firsthand that coming across as friendly and welcoming astronomically reduces anxiety and hugely increases the chances of having their

FLIRTING KNOWLEDGE QUIZ ANSWERS

1. **NO.** Even if you feel you weren't born with the "flirting gene," don't worry. Flirting is a talent that can be acquired and mastered, with styles that come in many flavors. With patience and practice, you'll find your groove.

2. **NO.** "Seduction" means coming on to someone in a sexual way. It is clear and direct, and might sound something like, "Hey babe, you really make me hot and bothered." Seduction is about one thing only—a sexual conquest.

3. **NO.** Flirting is honest and sincere: no power plays, no exploitation, no scheming.

4. **NO.** When flirting online, you can't rely on nonverbal cues to gauge reactions to your flirting.

5. **NO.** Really. A date isn't the goal—but the more you flirt, the greater your chances of getting a date. (More about this later.)

interest reciprocated. Flirting is a memorable way to make a connection with someone. And, if your flirting partner does not respond, your exit can be graceful and subtle because your approach was casual and understated.

- Flirting is a spectacular way to exude self-confidence and appear approachable and available.

- Flirting is the perfect way to let another person know that you exist so you can make a connection. And it can create an enticing atmosphere in which you can get to know each other.

- Flirting is synonymous with having fun, being playful, and acting natural.

- Flirting is a great way to let someone know you find him or her attractive, cool, witty, clever, well dressed, smart, or funny.

- Flirting is innocent banter between two people. The prize? Nothing more than the enjoyable interaction itself.

What is the Goal of Flirting?

The goal of flirting is to make the other person feel as if he or she is the most important person on the face of the planet. When you focus all of your attention on him and no one else, you're essentially telling him he's irresistible!

However, the goal of flirting is NOT to get a phone number or a date. Sorry to be the bearer of bad news! If your expectations go beyond the immediate encounter, you're setting yourself up for potential disappointment. But if your only objective is

DITCH THE JITTERS

Got a case of the nerves when you're about to approach your flirtee? (We've all been there.) Just remember this: There's no need to put her on a pedestal. She isn't a god: she's human. And she'll be delighted you approached her. You'll make her day!

to make someone feel special, you won't feel terribly disappointed if your flirtee does not respond in kind.

Ultimately, flirting is uplifting and enjoyable. As you flirt, you'll find yourself saying, "That made me feel great!" And, in turn, that'll give you the self-confidence (and desire) to flirt more often.

Flirting Fundamentals

Mastering the flirting fundamentals will make your flirting moves seamless and fabulous. In no time, they will become part of who you are and your flirting encounters will be better than you ever could have imagined!

- **Make flirting your new hobby:** Even if you're super busy. My guess is that you have more hobbies than you have time. Don't worry: You don't need to add another task to your busy day. Instead, do double duty! While you're shopping, walking the dog, commuting, grabbing lunch, browsing the bookstore, or sitting in the doctor's waiting room, I want you to make eye contact with, smile at, and start talking to strangers. I do this all the time. It makes the mundane stuff—like waiting in a long line—so much fun.

- **Talk to everyone.** Don't turn it on only when you are super attracted to someone. The downside of aiming exclusively for your mark is that you eliminate lots of potential opportunities in the process. The truth is that you just never know who your perfect match is—and you never know where a flirty conversation will take you. Perhaps your flirting partner is young enough to be your son or old enough to be your mom—but he or she may know a real cutie who's just right for you.

- **Find a wingwoman.** Having a wingwoman to inspire you can be lots of fun. So, pick a willing single friend, and schedule a flirting date at least once a week. Change venues each time and practice complimenting, initiating conversations, asking for help, or just commenting on the surroundings.

- **Be social wherever you are.** "Being social" is not a natural resource that you have to conserve, so let it flow. Some of us only turn on our "charming" personalities when he is right smack in front of us. But I want you to turn on your flirt all the time. If it's always part of you, you can kick it into high gear when Mr. Maybe Wonderful is sitting right next to you. After all, every loving relationship begins with that first conversation! Always remember that when you get the flirting jitters.

- **Never leave home without a prop**! They'll increase your chances of getting noticed and are natural conversation starters: They encourage and inspire others to talk to you. The best props are pets, kids, unusual jewelry, a fabulous scent, clothing with special meaning (such as your college sweatshirt; a T-shirt from a marathon you ran; a base-ball cap from Paris), or trendy or out-of-the-ordinary reading material.

» A cute pup can be the perfect flirting prop.

The Resilient Flirt

Overcoming the Fear of Flirting

The number one reason people choose not to flirt is the fear of rejection. Believe me. I get it. You don't want to get your feelings hurt. Fair enough. But take a moment to ask yourself: What are you so afraid of? You see a guy or gal who looks good to you, so you start a conversation and it goes nowhere. You feel bad—but what do you feel bad about? Is it that he doesn't like you? (He doesn't even know you.) Do you feel embarrassed that she knows you like her? (You don't even know her.) Do you think no one will ever like you? (That's a bit extreme—isn't it?) Or do you think he isn't responding to you because you're not pretty enough, not thin enough, or not___ enough? (Whichever adjective you choose, it's not true.)

One out of every three guys you approach is not going to be interested. That's the icy truth. So what's a gutsy, resilient flirt to do? Keep flirting, that's what. Just like dating, it's a numbers game: The more people you approach, the greater your chances of getting to yes.

The resilient flirt understands that the focus of flirting is the present moment. Your prospective flirting partner may or may not be interested. If he isn't, you've lost nothing, apart from this brief encounter; if he is, it may lead to something very, very special. Just like the lottery, you've got to be in it to win it.

Now, let's talk about how to maximize your chances of success when it comes to flirting!

Confidence is sexy. The most important component of successful flirting is self-confidence. When you radiate confidence, people will instantaneously be drawn to you. You become the person everyone wants to talk to because you skillfully put flirtees at ease. And a truly confident person doesn't have to prove her self-worth to others, nor is she constantly seeking approval and endorsements—she's comfortable with herself.

If your confidence quotient has plummeted post-breakup or divorce, don't worry. These tips can help you regain your self-confidence:

Envision your best-looking you. When you're in the dating market, you never know when an opportunity might present itself. Use that as an excuse to look your best. (Besides, when you feel irresistible, you are irresistible, and flirting will happen naturally when you're so self-assured.) Dig out a favorite photograph of yourself—this is the appearance you should take time to achieve. Consider bringing back the bangs you used to love, or buy another tube of that red lipstick you used to wear every Friday night.

The following tips can help you look your best:

- Take a makeup lesson. Lots of makeup counters do this for free when you buy a product or two. Or, get a talented friend to give you a tutorial.

- Shop for a couple of new outfits. Take a fashionista friend along: She'll give you an honest opinion on the styles that flatter you.

- Try contact lenses instead of glasses. It may take a couple attempts to put them in, but it's worth it! Alternatively, update your frames for a fun new style.

- Invest in a trendy haircut or a new color. Now's the time to visit that cool salon you walk past on your way to work!

- Get a facial—one of the best ways to pamper yourself, and you're left with glowing skin.

- Perfect your posture. Stand up tall with your tummy tucked in, your head high, and your chest out. You'll look taller and slimmer—and, more importantly, more self-assured.

- Get regular manicures. They're usually relatively quick, inexpensive, and can make you feel polished and elegant.

- Smell sensational. Treat yourself to your favorite perfume (or snag a free sample from a department store!).

- Complete your look with accessories such as jewelry, belts, and scarves: They're often easier on the wallet than a whole new outfit. Striking accessories can be great conversation pieces, too!

Fake it till you make it. This actually works! Acting as if you have self-confidence helps you feel better from the inside out—and the more you act the part, the more self-assured you become. The following tips can help boost your confidence. Practice them as often as possible!

- Think positive thoughts about yourself—even if you're not sure you believe them at first.

- Smile often. Scientific studies have shown that smiling actually produces positive feelings. (Plus, it makes you appear more open and approachable.)

- Maintain eye contact during a conversation.

CHUTZPAH AND CHARM

Flirting is a blend of one part chutzpah to three parts charm. Chutzpah, or "gutsiness," gives you the green light to be bold, brave, and fearless—and to take risks, too. It's what helps you make the first move, say hi, smile, and break free of your fear of rejection. Chutzpah also enables you to pick yourself up when the flirtee isn't interested: It doesn't let you give up. Think of chutzpah as the inner voice that gives you a push when you need it most. It's like skydiving: You might be afraid to jump, but once you take the plunge, it's the most exhilarating feeling.

- Listen attentively. Show you're engaged in what she's saying—lean toward her, ask questions, and refrain from interruptions.

- Show enthusiasm. It's infectious!

- Treat others as *they* want to be treated. Don't assume that everyone wants to be treated the same way you do; pay close attention to the cues he's sending.

- Laugh a lot. Not that you need to giggle non-stop—but, like enthusiasm, laughter is infectious, and it exudes positivity, too.

- Talk to strangers. The more you do this, the less scary it becomes. And you might make a few new friends along the way!

- Make small talk. Keep it upbeat, friendly, and light-hearted.

Skeptical? In my "How to Flirt" seminars, I ask participants to rate their feelings of self-confidence on a scale of 1 to 10 (with "1" being the lowest and "10" being the highest). Then, I ask if anyone who rated herself a 1 or 2 would like to become an 8 by the end of the class—of course, a number of hands shoot up. So, I select two or three participants who desperately want to boost their self-confidence. I ask them to leave the room, and I tell them that they are to take on the persona of, say, Beyoncé or Oprah, and to walk back into the class as if they had as much self-confidence as their chosen character. They are to greet the other students individually, telling each one how honored she is to meet them because of their heroic rescue efforts during a recent hurricane, and that her goal is to shine a spotlight on all of these heroes.

Well, the results were phenomenal. These shrinking violets, who had mumbled, blushed, and made little or no eye contact, were transformed into the most magnificent masters of ceremony imaginable. They were amazed at how incredible they felt while "pretending" they were assertive and self-assured—and they loved the positive reactions they got from the other students.

Charm is one part magnetism, two parts charisma, three parts warmth, and four parts authenticity—and it's also about being yourself. When you are charming, people are drawn to you because they feel sensational in your presence. Chutzpah propels you to take action, and charm is the beguiling attitude you need to be an out-of-the-ordinary flirt. What's the secret to radiating charm? Make the person you're talking to feel as if she is the most important person in the world. Remember, it's all about her—not you. It works every time—like a charm!

Your Body Language Says It All

In the "human jungle," the more you demonstrate flirtatious body language, the easier it is to make your move with confidence and the greater the likelihood that the guy you have your eye on will make his way over to you. Here's why: Everything you do with your body speaks volumes about how you are feeling and what you are thinking about the other person. According to a well-known study from 1967 by Professor Albert Mehrabian, in the dance of relationships, only 10 percent of your message is communicated through words alone. Ninety percent of your message is communicated through your facial expressions, eyes, voice, and gestures.

This means that using body language that signals you're approachable is by far the best way to catch the eye of a prospective flirtee. As proof, check out this scenario, which I'm sure you've seen played out in real life:

Five gorgeous gals sat down at one end of a bar. They wore scowls on their faces and expressions that practically screamed, "I'm better than you." At the other side of the bar sat five attractive women who were smiling, had open body language, looked happy, and moved to the music. The approachable women were surrounded by guys in no time, and the gorgeous gals were talking to–well, no one.

The more inviting your body language is, the more often you'll be approached. (How great is that?) So remember this fable the next time you find yourself feeling a bit nervous and insecure. Turn your taxi cab light on and send out your very own smoke signal so everyone knows you're approachable and welcome the attention.

One caveat: It is so important that your words and body language are in sync with each other. If they aren't, your flirting partner will respond exclusively to your nonverbal behavior. Here's an example: Rona was at a holiday party. She found herself at the dessert table juggling too many goodies and she dropped one of her cookies. Alex, who was standing next to Rona, quickly picked it up. Rona was appreciative, and the two started chatting. Alex started talking about how much he liked his new job, but at the same time he was pounding his fist into the palm of his other hand. Rona quickly excused herself because something about the gesture didn't feel right: "I'm just not believing this guy," she said to herself. Alex's words and actions definitely didn't match.

Flirtatious Body Language to Say You're Interested

Wouldn't it be fabulous if, when you notice someone at a party, a bar, in class, or at a coffee shop, you could send a note saying, "I think you're cute! Would you like to come over and get acquainted?" (And, of course, it'd be even greater if the person wrote back immediately with a resounding, "Yes! I'm on my way.") Well, this is exactly what body language achieves: It's a flirt's calling card. (No tacky pickup lines required.) Here's how to let your flirting partner know you think he or she is adorable:

SMILE

It's contagious! More than any other non-verbal signal, smiling communicates that you are approachable and easy to talk to. A smile is to flirting what air is to breathing: You can't have one without the other. The radiance and warmth of your smile will set the stage for graceful flirting—and it completely transforms your appearance. Ciara, a client of mine, just didn't understand that everything she was doing with her body language was preventing guys from approaching her. Then I asked her if I could take pictures of her when she was smiling and when she wasn't. When she saw how she looked "smileless," she got it. She couldn't believe how completely her face was transformed when she smiled. "I would never have approached me when I had that miserable look. I can't wait to put a smile on my face!"

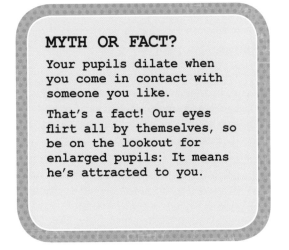

MYTH OR FACT?

Your pupils dilate when you come in contact with someone you like.

That's a fact! Our eyes flirt all by themselves, so be on the lookout for enlarged pupils: It means he's attracted to you.

Yes, a smile is universal; it is its own language. Without using words, it says, "I like you, I accept you, I am open to you, and I will not hurt you." The next time someone makes eye contact with you, return the eye contact with a huge smile. The best smile envelopes your entire face and shows off the beautiful crow's feet around your eyes. (That's right: They're beautiful!) And it takes forty-two muscles to frown, but only eight muscles to smile. That means it's easier to smile than not to.

MAKE EYE CONTACT

This is the very soul of flirting. Eye contact establishes trust and forges a connection instantaneously: It says you are interested in and attracted to your flirting partner. Eye contact communicates self-confidence, too, so say goodbye to shy, passive eye contact. Instead, bat your big brown, green, or baby blue peepers. The fun begins here!

To master eye contact:

- **Sneak a quick look (aka play peeka-boo).** Imagine you're at your favorite bookstore, and you see him on the other side of the shelf. You sneak a peek, then hide behind the shelf while you look at the books–and then you do it again. Try it once or twice, and on the second round, let your glance linger a bit. If you really want to be brave, walk over to him and say something like, "Hope you enjoyed our game of peeka-boo as much as I did!" He'll either be smiling from ear to ear or taken aback–but either way, you got his attention! (Of course, this is only an example: You can also peek over your glasses, a take-out menu, or anything you can "hide behind.") This is just about having fun and being playful. You're not being creepy–you're just a gal who wants to say hi.

- **"Smize."** Coined by supermodel Tyra Banks, "smize" means smiling with your eyes. According to Banks, "It is the secret to a perfect photo." So, let's apply Tyra's technique to flirting. Here's how expert smizers do it:

  ▶ Relax, take a deep breath, think happy thoughts, and feel your facial muscles loosen as you visualize something that brings a smile to your eyes.

  ▶ Focus on the flirtee. Keep your eyes steady and direct your attention to your flirting partner.

  ▶ Laugh out loud–or inwardly–simply because laughing makes your eyes come alive with enthusiasm.

  ▶ Let the smile start with your eyes and before you know it, you will have the perfect smize.

  ▶ Repeat these steps once or twice.

- **The glancing dance of the eyes.** This is my favorite technique because it's so easy and lighthearted. Simply glance at your flirting partner for a second or two, then look away. Repeat this once or twice. If you don't get the response you were hoping for, it's time to up the ante: Glance at your flirting partner for three to four seconds, then look away, and repeat two or three times if necessary.

- **Look and glance down.** This works like a charm when you're making eyes at someone from a distance. Look straight at her for about four seconds, then look down for about five seconds. Repeat if needed. Notice how her eyes will be waiting for yours when you look up again.

- **The art of winking.** A wink covers all the bases in a single maneuver. (How efficient is that?) A wink is a very private, intriguing, captivating, direct way to say, "Hey, you're my type." The closed eye of the wink also communicates a "secret" you are sharing, while the open eye conveys that the secret is not to be shared with anyone else in your line of vision.

Don't worry if you're not in the habit of winking–a little prep work is all that's required! As you look in the mirror, quickly close and open one eye as you look at yourself. See how you feel when you get winked at. Then pair the wink with a smize and a mysterious smile (that is, keeping your mouth somewhat closed). You might feel a bit awkward at first, but that's where your caring friend comes in. Rehearse your wink and ask for feedback. For instance, I find that I am a first-class winker with my right eye. But when I try to wink with my left eye—well, it just doesn't work. Once you're comfortable with it—and you will be!—a wink is a winning technique for breaking the ice with Mr. or Ms. Maybe Wonderful. Have fun!

PERFECT A FLIRTATIOUS HANDSHAKE

The goal of this handshake is to create warmth, energy, and intrigue, and there's nothing better for breaking the ice. Once you master it, you can replace your boring "business" handshake with a far more fun, flirtatious version.

Here's how to do it:

- Smile.
- Look directly at him.
- Move in toward him.
- Using your right hand, shake his hand in the ordinary way. But at the same time, fleetingly and softly, use your left hand to move your fingers gently across the back of his right hand. As you do so, say, "Hi, I'm (Your Name). I'm so pleased to meet you."

This handshake is so effective because you are reinforcing your engaging words with a brief, sensual touch—a winning combination that draws on a number of senses at once. You must try this: You'll be amazed at how well it works.

MOVE A LITTLE CLOSER

Get the sparks flying by creating the perfect distance between you and your flirtee. Your proximity to him is an extension of your body language, and it's key to the message you send: Too close, and you come across as overbearing and even a little creepy. Too far, and you'll lose his attention in a nanosecond!

How close is too close—and how far is too far? Here's a handy guide:

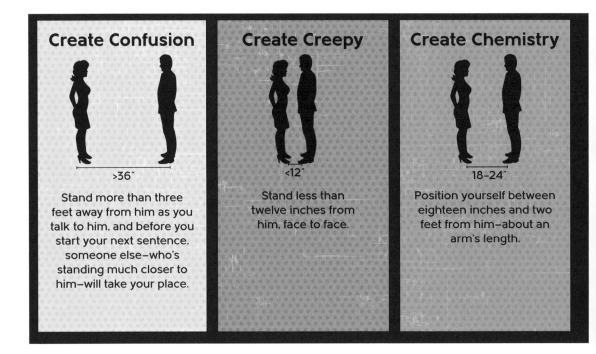

Create Confusion

>36"

Stand more than three feet away from him as you talk to him, and before you start your next sentence, someone else—who's standing much closer to him—will take your place.

Create Creepy

<12"

Stand less than twelve inches from him, face to face.

Create Chemistry

18-24"

Position yourself between eighteen inches and two feet from him—about an arm's length.

TOUCH YOUR FLIRTEE

Sparks are flying and the conversation is flowing: All is good in your flirting world! Now an accidental touch on his arm or hand will bring a wider smile to his face. Touch creates a sense of connection. As you're talking, don't be afraid to tap his arm as a way to agree with what he is saying, or to tap her hand when she says something you can relate to. One of the best times to touch is when you are sharing a laugh: It's the perfect time to touch him casually on the arm, shoulder, hand, or knee. The no-touch zones (for first-time flirting encounters, that is) include the face, head, and thigh. Just remember, use your touches sparingly to strengthen their effect. Avoid being too touchy-feely; it might make him uncomfortable.

Winning Opening Lines

Now that you've mastered flirtatious body language, you'll want to pair it with the right words. Let's talk about some great opening lines and conversation starters that are sure to kick off a great connection.

Your Friend, the Stranger

I was having breakfast at a local bagel shop. There were only two people in the whole place: me and a guy at a table right across from me. I was thinking about the best way to start a conversation with him when a light bulb went off in my head: I'd just talk to him as if I already knew him, instead of trying to come up with a one-liner, something funny, or a corny pickup line. Instantly I thought of tons of things to say, like, "Your omelet looks delish: What's in it?" or "I love going out for breakfast," or "I've never seen this place so empty," or "The staff here are so accommodating," or even, "Would you like company?" So, the next time you want to talk to a stranger, just talk about the obvious. You'll come across as natural and easy to talk to. (By the way, as soon as I was about to start chatting with him, he'd finished his meal and was heading for the door. The moral of the story? Don't delay!)

Butter Him Up

One of the best ways to start a conversation is to compliment your flirting partner. (Just make sure that what you say is authentic.) And the crème de la crème of compliments includes a hint of surprise. For instance, suppose you have ocean-blue eyes and get lots of compliments on them. Then imagine that a stranger compliments your cool jewelry, your scent, or your kindness in letting her step ahead of you in the checkout line. You may be used to receiving comments about your eyes–but you didn't see that one coming! In this way, the unexpected compliment really has the "wow" factor. So, let your imagination run wild when you are ready to dish out a compliment. Here are some examples:

He holds the door for you. You say, "What a gentleman! Your wife is so lucky to have you." (So what if he knows you're curious about his marital status?)

You love her perfectly coiffed hair. You say, "You have the most amazing hair. You are so lucky–and I am totally jealous!"

You love how put-together he looks. You say, "You have an incredible sense of style. Quite impressive!"

You see her walking her dog. You say with a smile, "You have such a well-behaved dog! I could really use your expertise. Can I hire you?"

Play a Game

It's hard to approach strangers, especially someone you think you might like. Make it into a game—everyone loves games, and it's certainly a novel way to break the ice. What I especially like about this approach is that it gives you a "reason" to have a conversation—even though you set it up. Plus, games add an element of intrigue and fun: What better way to get things going?

Game #1: Hi! I was trying to imagine what kind of work you do. Give me three choices and I'll guess.

Game #2: Excuse me, I just took a flirting class and my assignment was to introduce myself to the next handsome guy I saw. Hi, I'm (Your Name).

Game #3: I'm taking a survey on favorite foods. What are your top-five favorites?

Create Your Own Pickup Lines

I'm not a big fan of pickup lines because they make the flirtee feel as if the line is unoriginal or has been used dozens of times before. Plus, pickup lines can leave the flirtee speechless, and that's not the result you want.

But I have come across a few that can act as springboards for your creative opening lines. Practice saying them aloud and see how you feel hearing them, or try them out with a friend. The bottom line is, if it feels creepy, sounds cheesy, or if you cringe when you hear it, don't use it. Here are some samples: Even if you'd never use any of them, they might give you an idea for one of your own. (I'd love to hear your favorites, or what happens when you use any of these! Visit frangreene.com and keep me posted.)

I hope you know CPR . . . because you take my breath away.

Do you have a bandage? I just scraped my knee falling for you.

Do you like raisins? How do you feel about a date?

Do you believe in love at first sight—or should I walk by again?

It's a good thing I have my library card, because I am totally checking you out.

If you were on Tinder I would swipe right.

Oh, and if you want to use any of these in real life, you can always preface them with, "I have a few opening lines I'm going to try out on you." (In case the delivery doesn't go well, here's a lifesaver you can grab onto: "Sorry. That was awful! I just lost a bet with a friend and she made me give you the most pathetic pickup line I could think of." The delivery is the most important thing about any opening line. Don't take yourself too seriously! Have fun with it.)

Now that you are on 24/7 flirt alert, I'm going to show you how to visit the places you go every day with a flirty attitude.

Get Out There and Flirt Everywhere

Flirt Alert Venue #1: The Waiting Game

You already know that I love multitasking, and there's no better way to multitask than by flirting while you're waiting in line. You have the time, a common bond (you're both waiting for the same service), and you can transform an ordinary chore into an extraordinary opportunity. And you'll probably get the chance to do this at least once a day. Once you try this a couple times, you'll see how easy it is. A good way to begin is by chatting about what you already have in common—the line you're standing in.

For instance:

Play a game. "Let's bet on how long the wait is going to be. The loser lets the winner go first—or the winner buys coffee afterward!"

Pay a compliment. "You have so much patience with this long line. How long have you been waiting?"

Smile and make eye contact as if to say hello. "This restaurant must be a real hot spot—the line is so long. I've never been here before. Have you?"

Flirt Alert Venue #2: The Food Frenzy

Food is a natural conversation starter. You can hit it off with your flirting partner while bantering about the latest diet craze, the rebirth of cauliflower, chocolate pizza, your favorite item on the menu, or by commenting on the items in her shopping cart. Some of the best settings for this include food courts, snack bars, take-out counters, restaurants, food stores, specialty food shops, neighborhood restaurants, farmers' markets, fast-food restaurants, coffee shops, or ice cream shops.

If you're at the supermarket, be on the lookout for solo shoppers. When you spot one, ask her a question about something she's selected, or comment on an item in her cart:

Seek his expertise. "I never know how to choose a ripe watermelon. You look watermelon savvy: Any thoughts?"

Ask for a hand. "Would you mind reaching that can of soup for me? Thanks for being tall! No–thanks for being at the right place at the right time!"

Or, as you're waiting in line at any self-service restaurant, jump at the chance to show your interest in the cutie next to you:

"So many cupcakes to choose from and they all look so good! Such a hard decision: What do you suggest?"

"I never know what to order here: What do you get?" Wait for an answer, then reply: "That sounds delicious: I'll get that. Thanks so much. Hopefully I can return the favor sometime."

Flirt Alert Venue #3: The Social Butterfly

Social events offer the best backdrop for the active flirt. The vibe is bubbly, convivial, and upbeat. Some of the best events for flirting include birthdays, holidays, office parties (carefully), engagement celebrations, cocktail parties, retirement parties, weddings, religious celebrations, school reunions, barbeques, and smaller, more informal gatherings of all sorts.

Accept all the social invitations you can. It makes life interesting, and it gives you a chance to try out your newly acquired flirting skills. Of course, if you're suddenly single and socializing alone, all sorts of what-ifs can rear their ugly heads. What if they ask where my boyfriend is–or what if everyone is part of a couple?

Don't freak out and ditch your plans. Instead, just be prepared. For example:

Be honest.

Q: "Where's your boyfriend?"

A: "We're not together anymore." Or "I'm in the dating market. What about you?"

Get comfortable with couples.

Q: What if everyone is part of a couple?

A: They probably won't be. Chances are, you won't be the only single person there–and if you are, so what? Practice your flirting skills; make playful, fun connections with no intentions other than making your flirting partner feel special. You can flirt with anyone–whether they're single or not.

Challenge yourself.

Decide to talk to ten people over the course of the event. Introduce yourself to the other guests: Ask how they know the host, whether they're tried any of the food, or how far they traveled to the event, for instance.

Bring your business cards.

Always have a business card on hand just in case you want to exchange phone numbers with someone. (If you don't have a business card, create a "personal" card with your name and contact info.) Feel a little funny having a calling card that isn't business? No problem: When designing yours, consider a general title such as "Entrepreneur," "Self-Employed," "Gourmet Cook," "Marathon Runner," "Spelling Bee Champion," "Consultant," or "Writer."

Flirt Alert Venue #4: Get that Heart Pumping

Any activity that boosts your heart rate is good for flirting. Why? When you exercise, your brain releases endorphins, which are hormones that actually make you feel happier. So take advantage of your good mood–and of the bond you have with other exercisers–while you're walking your pooch, jogging, attending exercise class, working out at the gym, doing martial arts, or dancing. Or, join a biking, hiking, golf, tennis, or swimming club: These are social by their very nature.

Breaking the ice with a fellow "athlete" is so simple it's a dream come true. Since you already have much in common, your opening line will be seamless and natural. Here's how to flex your flirting muscles:

At the gym:

"I could use your help figuring out this machine. I noticed you are a pro at it."

"Any suggestions for an easy exercise for my abs? I couldn't help noticing yours."

As you leave the gym, say, "Have a great day. See you soon." Then, the next time you see him, say, "Hi, great to see you again! I don't think we've met: I'm (Your Name)."

Walking the dog:

Don't walk your dog just anywhere! Visit a place where other dog walkers go regularly such as a public park or a dog park. And always talk to the other dog first, before you address its owner. It's such a natural transition: It makes talking to the dog walker so much easier. (It's just like oohing and aahing at a baby!)

If you don't have a dog, borrow one: They're natural conversation starters. Here are some useful opening lines, and they're so simple:

"What an adorable dog."

"What's your dog's name? (pause) My dog's name is Brutus."

"Do you and your dog come here often?"

Flirt Alert Venue #5: Away You Go!

Whether you're commuting to work or flying halfway around the world, travelling offers great opportunities for flirting. After all, travelling can be long and boring, but flirting will make the time fly, and you can meet some very interesting people en route. When you're on the go, you can flirt at airports or on airplanes; on commuter trains; at bus stops; at tourist attractions; in hotel lobbies or bars; or on singles' vacations.

Of course, when you're travelling far from home, sometimes you have to seize the day and just flirt with someone right away because you might never see her again. I'm reminded of a story about a news reporter who was riding the subway in New York City. He saw a beautiful woman get off the train. While the train was still at the stop, he knocked on the window and mouthed, "Will you marry me?" The woman quickly got back on the train and said, "What did you say?!" He said, "I had to

do something to get your attention!" And the best part of the story is that they did get married. So, be prepared to be bold, or you might miss your chance.

Here are some make-the-first-move questions perfect for travelers or commuters:

Ask for directions. "Excuse me, but do you get off at the next stop for the art museum?"

Ask for help with your luggage. "Would you mind getting that purple suitcase down from the overhead rack? I can't quite reach it. (pause) Thank you so much!"

Ask for a restaurant suggestion. "I've never been to [Chicago/New York/Kansas City] before: Can you recommend a good place to eat?"

Commiserate about travel delays and grab a bite to eat. "I can't believe we're delayed another two hours! I might grab a burger. Would you like to join me?"

Share your travel war stories. "This delay actually isn't too bad. Once I was stranded in L.A. for ten hours! What about you?"

Talk about your travel experiences. "I love travelling, but I think my favorite place in the world is Paris. What's yours?"

Flirt Alert Venue #6: Shop till You Drop

Shopping and flirting go hand in hand. So why not go on a flirting shopping spree? (You don't actually have to buy anything: All you need to do is be ready to flirt!) As you shop, be sure you're smiling, making eye contact, and walking with confidence. Spend a couple hours or an afternoon at the bookstore, the mall, outlet stores, a department store, or your local mom-and-pop shop. Take your time and wander around. When you see a good-looking guy, chat about the sales, the crowds, or ask his opinion about the gadget you're looking at. Or, ask him to recommend a good place to eat. If you are getting the flirting vibe back, ask him if he'd like to join you.

"Have you ever read John Grisham? I love crime fiction, but I've never read anything by him."

"Excuse me, but I can't remember which way the food court is: Can you point me in the right direction?"

"I need to buy a present for my brother. Would you go for this shirt in blue or black?"

Flirt Alert Venue #7: Pay it Forward

Consider volunteering. Giving back is great for the giver, and it's a blessing for those on the receiving end. You're doing a good deed and you also have the opportunity to meet other people who believe in the same causes. Have fun flirting while enriching the lives of others; it's a win-win.

Comment on the activity you're doing together, but stay positive. "I can't believe we've walked seven miles already! Time has flown, hasn't it? My name's _____, by the way."

Help each other. Smile, then say: "Could you pass me those bowls? (pause) Thanks so much! Now all I have to do is to keep from dropping them . . . !"

Ask her opinion. "How many pencils should we include in each backpack? Or do you think the kids need more pens instead?"

Flirt Alert Venue #8: Get a Breath of Fresh Air

Being outdoors encourages flirting because there's so much activity going on around you. Check out people-packed places—they're full of people to talk to! Be on the lookout for someone who looks approachable and friendly. Smile, make eye contact, and get the conversation going.

At a street fair:

"Have you tried the fried dough from this place? It smells amazing!"

At the ice rink:

"I haven't skated in years, but I can't wait to try it again! I'll probably fall a hundred times, though. What about you? You look pretty steady on your feet!"

At an outdoor bar:

"There's a great view from here. I wonder what it's like at sunset?"

No matter where you are, flirting opportunities will always present themselves. It's up to you to be on flirt alert! Vary the when, the where, and the how—but make sure you're a full-time flirt, focused on making fun connections with new people. Life will be so much more exciting!

Digital Flirting

Now that you've mastered the world of offline flirting, it's time to go online. The rest of this chapter is an up-to-the-minute course in flirting in the digital world. Don't worry if you haven't done much digital flirting: It's easy, and, in no time, you'll be helping all your newly single girlfriends, too. We don't have room for a full social media course here, but let's review the essential points of using Facebook; flirting via text, instant messages, and email; crafting social media profiles; and selecting a profile photo.

Facebook and Dating

At the time of writing, almost 2 billion people are active Facebook users. It's a great way to widen your social circle, so you might want to send friend requests to friends from high school or college, friends you met on vacation, neighbors, former colleagues, family members, or your kid's friends' parents, to name a few.

The best reason to have a lot of friends on Facebook is that you get to see friends of your friends, and if someone catches your eye, you can ask your friend to arrange an old-fashioned introduction. But, when it comes to friending your date(s) on Facebook, be cautious. Things can get pretty messy if you friend someone too soon. You want him to get to know you in real life, not through your social media presence.

Creating events on Facebook is another opportunity to meet someone new. For instance, a dinner cruise event was organized for West Point cadets and an au pair's organization. Jana commented on a post George made and they decided to meet half an hour before the event began. They dated, fell in love, got married, and are now the proud parents of a baby boy. Jana said, "If I hadn't responded to his post, who knows if we'd ever have connected at the event?" George said, "I never knew my post about motion sickness would lead to the happiest day of my life."

Flirting via Texting

Flirting via texting is a quick, playful way to communicate interest, and it utilizes the dynamic duo of offline flirting and texting. And it has pros and cons. On one hand, you can take your time to craft your flirty text, which you can't do when you're flirting in person–but on the other, you can't rely on body language or tone of voice to gauge how your text is being received. It's a handy tool, but keep the following tips in mind–especially when your thumbs are working faster than your brain!

- **Use emoticons selectively.** The fewer you use, the greater the effect, because emojis communicate feelings.

- **Dare to be different.** Avoid texting shorthand. Instead, use punctuation, proper grammar, and correct spelling. (Too much shorthand can be a bit distracting, and can easily be misinterpreted in the getting-to-know-you phase.)

- **Make sure you send the flirty text to the intended person.** Rookie mistake!

- **Does your text make you smile?** If your text puts a smile on your own face, that's a good sign. She's sure to have fun reading it, too.

- **Trust your gut.** You'll know that your text is well crafted and ready to go when the thought of pressing "send" makes your stomach do flip-flops in anticipation of an instantaneous flirty response!

- **Be yourself.** Your texting style should mimic your in-person flirting approach. If you would never say it offline, don't say it via text.

When should you send a flirty text—and how will your flirtee interpret it? These guidelines will help:

● **Right after you exchange phone numbers.** Drop her a line and say something simple like, "It was so much fun talking to you tonight. Looking forward to seeing you again."

Implied message: If you ask me out, I'll say yes!

● **When your matchmaker sets you up.** If your matchmaker friend gives you a potential match's phone number, text him and tell him who you are and that you'd love to meet for a drink or a cup of coffee. He'll be so flattered.

Implied message: I'm super confident and not afraid to make the first move.

● **When she least expects to hear from you**—for example, when she knows you're away on a business trip. This is a surefire way to let her know she's on your mind (and in your heart).

Implied message: *I can't stop thinking about you.*

● **After a first date.** Send him a thank-you text, like, "The dinner was delicious, the wine was fabulous, and your smile melted my heart!" (Be sure that your message sounds and feels unique to you.)

Implied message: I had a great time; I like you!

● **To suggest a second date.** A flirty text is a safe way to test the dating waters—that is, to see if she is interested in date number two. For instance, "*Casablanca* is showing next Sunday, and I've never seen it. I'd love to see it with you."

Implied message: I can't wait to see you again.

FACEBOOK MESSAGING

Private messages (PMs) are a perfect way to let someone know you only want to flirt with him or her, not the entire Facebook world. It'll make him feel special, and can lead to exchanging phone numbers. If you don't get a response after your initial PM, send another one. Make sure your tone is upbeat and relaxed.

Not sure what to say if he didn't message you back? Don't point out that he didn't respond. Instead, say something like, "Hey____, I was thinking about you and hope you got my message from the other day. If you didn't [you're letting him off the hook], and I know that can happen, I'd still love to try that new make-your-own pizza place. Let me know if you're up for that."

INSTANT MESSAGING

Instant messaging is the closest thing to a real-life conversation, so treat it as if you were talking to him on the phone. The expectation is that you will respond instantaneously to his message, so you'll have to think on your feet and go with the flow. It's okay to give yourself a few seconds to compose your thoughts before you type, but it's best to be brief and concise.

Because your flirting partner can see when you're online, don't disappear into thin air; instead, when you want (or have to) end the "conversation," say, "I have to run to a meeting," or "I'm at the dentist and I have to go in now, so let's continue this in about an hour." Otherwise he will think you are giving him radio silence, and we all know that's not a good thing! Emojis really enhance your IMs, so use them to add some excitement or intrigue.

Flirting Online Using E-Mail/Messages

Cyber flirting is a fabulous way to build rapport, make a connection, and demonstrate playfulness and intrigue. In the off-line world you can wink, smile, move in closer, laugh, pay compliments, and show your flirting interest that he has captured your heart. In the online world, all you have are your onscreen words, so you'll have to be extra-creative with them. (Still, at times, flirting online can actually be simpler, because you have the luxury of taking your time and crafting your message or response.) Here's how to master the art of flirting online when you're crafting that perfect email to your "potential date" on an online dating site, or the guy you met on the train, or the gal you reconnected with at a recent high school reunion.

USE EMOTICONS

Think of emoticons as new and improved punctuation. They are the perfect way to add flavor and interest to your words—in the same way that smiling, changing the inflection of your voice, or brushing against his arm does. Experiment with them: Send yourself an email without emoticons, and then send yourself one with them. Do you have a different reaction to the two emails? Do the emoticons change the intent of your words? (Use this technique as a guide: Your response is likely to be similar to his.) Emoticons are also a safe way to express an emotion or a thought that you might be a bit hesitant to share in words—like a heart, a wink, or a kiss.

PERFECT YOUR PUNCTUATION

Your message is communicated through your nonverbal behavior—so how's a flirty gal like you going to do that online? Here's how to spice up your emails (or social media conversations) and get noticed every time.

- When you use an exclamation point(s), you demonstrate enthusiasm and excitement.

  My mouth is watering just thinking about that hot and sour soup!!

- Strategically placed ellipses are very alluring, intriguing, and add an air of mystery.

  Would love to hear all the details about your trip to Iceland . . .

- Using capital letters reveal passion, excitement, and positivity.

  I am SOOOO looking forward to getting a rescue dog from the shelter.

- Parentheses are a good way to add interest and curiosity (and clever asides) to your messages.

  I am so impressed (you are amazing) that you make peanut butter and jelly sandwiches for the homeless.

- Abbreviations and symbols add fun and playfulness.

  You made me ☺ when you talked about your daughter.

  I was LOL-ing when I read your comments about your golf game because I could so relate to it.

AIM FOR A CHATTY TONE

When you're writing to your "mystery date," you want her to feel like you're talking to her in the same way you would in person. You want her to feel relaxed and interested and to smile as she reads your message.

NO NOVELS, PLEASE

A short email will go a long way. Write just enough to let him get a glimpse of who you are and what you are looking for. And always show interest in him by asking questions. When you don't know someone well, long emails are boring. So, don't go on and on: He'll hit delete just seconds after you finish your autobiography.

Social Media Profiles

Social media is another great way to expand your flirting expertise—and to connect with friends of friends whom you wouldn't have the opportunity to meet otherwise. Here are my favorite social media flirting tips.

- **Craft an eye-catching social media profile.** Take the time to make your profile unique and reflective of who you are. But keep it succinct and concise.

- **Attract "single prospects."** Edit your privacy settings to allow the public to see your profile pictures, relationship status, the schools you attended, mutual friends, your bio, your favorite quotes, or headline. Also, edit your privacy settings to allow the "public" to send you messages or friend requests.

- **Be honest** and let your personality shine through. As for status updates and the items you share, remember that over-sharing is not flirty; instead, it screams "irritating" and "overkill." Change up your photos regularly, share links and articles you're passionate about, and always be upbeat, positive, and playful.

- **Get personal.** When sending a friend request, add a personal message, especially if you don't know the person directly. Remind her of your connection.

- **Be selective about liking his stuff.** Selectively and sparingly liking his posts and photos will get you noticed. Don't click "like" on posts that are more than two weeks old: You'll look like you're "cyber stalking."

PROFILE PHOTO PREP

If you're feeling a bit insecure in the looks department (and who hasn't been there?) consider investing in some professional photos, or get a photographer friend to take a few good shots. Wear your favorite top, take extra time with hair and makeup, and have fun: Your photo shoot will boost your confidence enormously! Then, on your profile, include pictures that encourage questions or comments—ones that reveal your varied interests, the places you've traveled to, and your unique personal spirit. (Skip drunken, overly revealing photos, or any that feature former significant others.)

- **Be brief.** When you're commenting on her posts, stick to a sentence or two. Think of your comments as the written, digital counterpart to in-person small talk and eye contact. Say just enough to get noticed and inspire a response: long, drawn-out comments are huge turnoffs. (And guess what? She's not going to read them.)

- **Follow photo etiquette.** Your profile image speaks volumes about who you are. Puppy photos, movie star photos, silly caricatures—or no photos at all–will raise a few questions. Are you hiding something? Do you think you're unattractive? If you have an active Facebook profile, why are you so invested in being private?

Flirting is an amazing way to make connections both online and offline. And now it's time to put those skills to work!

You are never too old to set another goal or to dream a new dream.

-C.S. LEWIS,
NOVELIST

MASTER IT: Unlock the Secrets of Online Dating

Step back in time with me for a moment to 1986. If you were dating then, you might remember personal ads—a revolutionary way for singles to meet each other by placing advertisements in print newspapers and magazines. Personal ads usually appeared once a week and they looked something like this:

"SCF [single Christian female] 36 seeks SDCM [single, divorced Christian male]) 35 to 45 who is financially, physically, and emotionally fit. If you like piña coladas and walks on the beach, let's meet."

The only way to contact the love-seeker was to write a note to him or her and include your phone number—and, possibly, a photo.

Can you imagine how time-consuming that was? Plus, the pickings tended to be slim: at best, there were only about five personal ads you'd even consider responding to. But singles just like you did it all the time, and they spent hours writing endless letters to an ad that would only run for one week—an ad that cost the advertiser around $150 to place, by the way. (And to make matters worse, you only had six weeks to respond to a personal ad.)

The single men and women of 1986 would have done anything to gain access to the zillions of dating sites and apps that you take for granted! And statistics show that it works. According to a 2012 study by the University of Chicago, more than one-third of couples who married met online.

And in 2010, a study conducted by Stanford University found that online dating is the second most common way for couples to meet.

Dating sites and apps are an awesome way to gently dip your toes in the dating pool; to embark on a full-on husband-finding mission; or to find a happy medium between those two extremes. In this step, I'm going to show you how to maximize your success and minimize your disappointments. I'll guide you through every step of the process, even if you've never used online dating before, or if you're trying it again after having stepped away from it for a while.

Dating sites and apps are changing faster than the speed of light. New ones pop up all the time and others fall by the wayside. I'll make reference to some specific, well-known sites and apps throughout this step, but this is just for the purpose of explanation. Some sites may have changed by the time you read this.

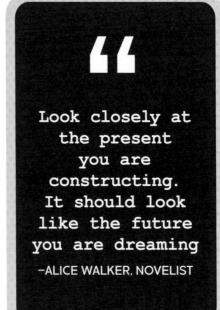

> **" Look closely at the present you are constructing. It should look like the future you are dreaming**
>
> —ALICE WALKER, NOVELIST

Online Dating Sites
What's Not to Love?

Just like anything else, online dating can be a blessing or a curse—depending on the way in which you approach it. So let's focus on the positive! Here's why you should love online dating sites.

It Doesn't Have to Cost You a Dime (Really!)

Yes, there are dating sites that don't charge their users. So, if your number one reason not to take the plunge and try it (or to try it again) is the cost, you can't use that as an excuse. And if you're ambivalent about online dating, (and who isn't?) the "free" factor can be a win-win: There's no financial risk involved in giving it a shot.

I used to think that free sites should be avoided, because anyone who was "really looking" for a relationship would only use a paid site. But after interviewing many women who met their husbands or boyfriends on free sites such as Plenty of Fish and OKCupid, I changed my mind. You don't necessarily need to subscribe to a paid online dating site—even if you're looking for a serious relationship.

 Online dating secret: *Join a free site and a site that charges a fee.* Why? Because signing up for two sites will increase your chances of success. And when you pay for something, you have a psychological investment in it, which means you will work harder at it because you want to get your money's worth. (That's just human nature!) Therefore, users of paid sites may be equally as committed—or even more committed—to finding love as you are, and that's a good thing for sure! (P.S.: If you sign up for a paid site and don't pay right away—paid sites do allow nonpaying members to browse and receive some correspondence—the site is likely to send you discounted offers as time goes on. You can also try negotiating the price with the site, or you can ask about special offers. This works: Clients of mine have been able to get a discounted rate just by asking.)

No Matter Who You Are, There's a Site Just for You

In 2013, *Online Dating Magazine* estimated that there were 2,500 online dating sites in the United States and about 5,000 worldwide—and this figure has only increased with time. This means that, even if you think online dating isn't for you, there are sites that will resonate with you because you already have something in common with the other members. There are oodles of niche sites that cater to a very specific group of singles: to find one you like, all you have to do is Google "dating," plus your interest, passion, religion, ethnicity, or hobby, and see what pops up. I tried it myself, and came up with these examples:

If you are gluten free:
www.glutenfreesingles.com

If you can't live without golf:
www.dateagolfer.com

If you are tall: www.tallfriends.com

If you only want to date someone Jewish:
www.JDate.com

If you love motorcycles:
www.bikerkiss.com

If you are older than fifty:
www.seniorpeoplemeet.com

If you want to go on a date doing something you love ASAP:
www.howaboutwe.com

Of course, you don't necessarily need to target someone with exactly the same interests as yours. Here are three "mainstream" sites that simply focus on matching compatible people:

www.match.com: Match.com claims to be "responsible for more dates, relationships, and marriages than any other online dating site." It's in twenty-four countries, has websites in fifteen languages, and has a huge membership—probably the largest in the world. They offer a free seven-day trial; they guarantee that if you don't find someone special in six months, you get six months free; and, if you sign up for a premium membership, Match allows you to talk and text anonymously using a product called matchPhone. Those are some serious advantages.

www.zoosk.com: Zoosk is available in twenty-five languages and has subscribers all over the world. The site provides you with a daily introduction and also sends you a "carousel "of photos on which you can click "yes" or "no." It also has a virtual coin system, which allows you to purchase coins that will get your profile featured, and to send virtual gifts to prospective dates.

www.eharmony.com: eHarmony claims to be responsible for more than 500 marriages each day. All members must fill out an extensive, time-consuming questionnaire. Matches are then made based on "29 key dimensions" that predict relationship success. It is an ideal site if you're looking for a serious commitment or marriage. But the downside is you can't search for your own matches.

I wish there were a simple formula for selecting a mainstream dating site. Since there isn't, the best advice I can give you is to do your research before you decide. Read about them and ask friends for recommendations before you select the site that feels best for you.

💬 **Online dating secret:** *Join a niche site and a mainstream site.* Mainstream sites have the added value of a large membership base, giving you tons of potential matches to choose from. But, although niche sites have a significantly smaller number of members, your shared interests and values make up for that because you already have something in common with potential matches.

Not All the Good Ones are Taken!

It's true. So many guys: so little time. And how else—apart from online sites and apps—could you possibly be introduced to so many potential dates? After all, online dating is a continuous, never-ending, constantly changing supply of eligible men and women who want to date—and it's pretty hard to beat that!

Plus, online dating gives you the opportunity to meet someone you'd never ordinarily meet otherwise. You can search for someone who's a single parent; someone who lives within forty miles of you; someone who wants to have kids, just like you; or someone who shares your love of French cuisine and scuba diving. You can filter in (or out) just about anything you do or don't want.

💬 **Online dating secret:** *Visit several dating sites* and read the success stories. They're uplifting and encouraging and are sure to inspire you.

There Aren't Enough Hours in the Day

Dating often takes a back seat when your life is already overbooked. Do you have a demanding job with long hours? Are you studying for your master's degree and working at the same time? Are you a single parent? Do you work two jobs? Or do you care for an aging parent?

No matter how busy your schedule is, online dating can fit into it. You can search the web for your dream guy or gal at 6 a.m. or 11 p.m.; during your lunch hour; while you're in the dentist's waiting room; when your kids are out with your ex—basically, any time and any place. For instance, if you find yourself alone on a Friday night, what better way to make use of your down time than to go "shopping" for a date? Or, are you too tired to go to a club with your friends on Saturday night after working a twelve-hour shift? No problem: Change into a cozy pair of sweats, order in some sushi, then search, swipe, and click away till the sun comes up (or until you conk out on the couch!).

💬 **Online dating secret:** *Challenge yourself to "wink," "like," "flirt," or "give a thumbs-up" to at least fifty potential dates.* (These features were designed so you can let him know that he's caught your eye—without having to say a word!)

It Saves Time and Money

These days, there's a website for just about anything you're looking for. If you're anything like me, you probably do plenty of research on the best travel deals, the best restaurants, the most highly recommended doctors, and the most reliable cars before you make a purchase. So, why not use technology to find love in the same way you search for everything else? Plus, being on the "prowl" is expensive and time-consuming, and doesn't often yield results—despite your best efforts.

Heidi, for example, one of my clients, told me, "I rushed home from work to prepare for my evening out. It was a hot summer night and I was exhausted, so I decided the best way to prepare for my 'big night out on the town' was to get a mani-pedi, and to have my long locks blown out. Since I didn't have a car, I took an Uber to the club. I had no time to eat, so I grabbed a bite before I got to the club, and I ordered two drinks during my night out. It was a great night, but I didn't meet anyone I had any interest in. So I went home empty-handed—after I shelled out all that money. (P.S.: I got a ride home with a friend.) I could have spent that on an online dating membership. I am signing up for one first thing in the morning—after a cup of coffee! But don't get me wrong: I will still go out with my friends. It's all about creating balance and variety in my social life."

♥ **Online dating secret:** *The cost of joining an online dating site is not expensive, it's priceless.*

It's a Singles' Bar Open 365 Days per Year

Is there a singles' bar in your neighborhood open 24/7, every day of the year? There is—and it's in your smartphone. This might come as a huge relief: If you're the type who hides in the corner of the coolest bar in town, sipping a single apple martini for three hours, the likelihood of you meeting anyone is pretty slim! Think of your phone as a made-to-order singles' bar that suits your personality perfectly. You can wink, flirt, give a thumbs-up, and like his photo—while sipping a glass of pinot grigio on the couch with your feet up! You might even get a thumbs-up, a wink, or a flirt in return before the night is over.

♥ **Online dating secret** *Dating sites and apps are perfect venues for being the fabulous flirt you are!*

Picture Perfect
Pick a Profile Photo

On online dating sites and apps, the single most important part of your profile is your photo. Profiles with a photo get at least eight times as much traffic as a "blank" profile. And selecting your online photos can trigger a ton of anxiety. Maybe the reality that you're putting yourself out there (what fabulous news!) has just hit you; maybe you worry that everyone else is more attractive than you are (not likely); or perhaps you're embarrassed that someone you know might see you (if so, you're both in the same boat–and besides, you might be a perfect match!).

All you need are three to six photos that capture your spirit, your great smile, your authenticity, and you doing the things you love. Flaunt what you are proud of–such as the 10k run you did last month–and downplay the things you're most reluctant to show off to your prospective matches.

We already talked about choosing a photo for your social media profiles. Use what you learned to select photos for your dating profile. Here are some other helpful hints:

Photo Opportunity #1: Save the Best for First

Your photos are the most valuable real estate in your online dating portfolio. I know I've said it before, but I'll say it again: You only have one shot to make a lasting impression. So the first photo your poten-

tial match sees should be your very best shot. Pick the photo you love the most– the one that makes you feel great about yourself. Then, recruit a guy or gal friend–someone similar in age to the guy/gal you are searching for–and ask for help. Show him your nine favorite photos and ask him to pick his top three. Make sure he knows you want him to be totally honest. (You make the final decision if the two of you disagree.)

Photo Opportunity #2: It's All about the Numbers

According to eHarmony, posting four photos was the magic number for getting responses from potential dates. Most online daters agree that posting more than seven photos is way too many, and actually pushes potential matches away. But I think a total of six photos is perfect. They should include your best shot; one full body shot; two action/activity shots; one flirty shot; and one that highlights your smile.

Not quite sure how to create a flirty shot? Here's some inspiration for your next photo shoot: Imagine you've spotted a really cool guy across the room, and you think he's adorable. Smile at him and use approachable, welcoming body language plus some alluring eye contact.

Photo Opportunity #3: Don't Skip the Full Body Shot

When it comes to attraction, everyone has a "type"—or, at least, thinks they do. For instance, you may be super thin and athletic, but his "type" is a more voluptuous, curvy gal. Well, if thin and trim turns him off, it's better that he doesn't click on your profile. But on the other hand, your photo just might change his mind! He might think he knows what his type is, until he sees your photo, and can't wait to click on it.

That's why full disclosure is always best. Plus, imagine how awful this would be: Let's say your photos don't capture the way you really look in person. Then, when your date sees you in real life, she gasps in surprise. That's not a good way to start a first date—for either one of you. So, as the saying goes, honesty is the best policy. Post a full body shot of yourself that actually looks like you.

Photo Opportunity #4: Actions Speak Louder than Words

OKCupid founder Christian Rudder says the photos that spark the most conversations are pictures that showcase people doing something interesting. So, include pictures that will pique his curiosity or give her an opportunity to see you doing what

you love—such as playing an instrument, visiting a historical site, cooking your favorite meal, giving your pooch a bath, taking a kayak lesson, standing on the balcony of a ship with a glacier behind you, teaching sign language, knocking down a wall in your house, or anything else that provides a glimpse of what makes you unique. These are the best conversation starters.

Photo Opportunity #5: Flirt with the Camera

Imagine you're looking into the eyes of the most amazing guy or gal on the face of the planet. Smile, make eye contact, and—if you can pull it off—include a photo in which you're winking, since it's a great way to appear warm, inviting, happy, and confident. After all, he wants to imagine you as a gal he can have fun with—someone who'll enhance his life.

Photo Opportunity #6: Show off Your Left Side

According to a study conducted by Wake Forest University in 2012, the left side of your face is perceived as more pleasant than the right side of your face. Researchers say this is because we display more emotion on the left sides of our faces. Try it and see for yourself!

Photo Opportunity #7: Avoiding Photo Fails

✘ No suggestive or sexual pics. Sexually suggestive photos suggest you're not looking for anything serious. Keep it classy and keep your clothes on. (A little cleavage is okay as long as it's tasteful.)

✘ No pictures of you and your ex.

✘ No group pictures (with one exception: if the group is participating in an unusual activity or event that's essential to showing off your personality. In that case, go ahead–just be sure to identify yourself in the photo's caption.)

✘ No more than one photo of yourself in sunglasses.

✘ Never post only a single pic of yourself. (It suggests you only have one decent shot of yourself or that your photo is too good to be true.)

✘ No photos that are too dark, too light, or blurry.

✘ No pictures with your kids or parents.

✘ No photos in which someone has been cut out.

✘ No bathroom selfies.

✘ Don't sit or stand in the same pose in all photos.

✘ No photos older than eighteen months.

How to Craft the (Almost) Perfect Profile

When it comes to writing, rewriting, and obsessing over every word in your profile, the best-kept secret is this: Your profile is a work in progress—unlike your professional resume, which you get only one chance to send to a potential interviewer. Your username, headline, and profile can all be tweaked whenever you want, and you have as many do-overs as your love-seeking heart desires. In fact, making changes to your profile scores higher rankings on some sites. So don't overthink it: That'll only make the whole process feel overwhelming.

You don't have to create your profile all alone. Ask a friend for help—ideally, someone who's a great storyteller or writer. She or he will often be able to articulate amazing things about you that you might have overlooked. You can also enlist the services of online dating coaches who specialize in writing online profiles.

For many people, the most agonizing part of the whole process is writing the open-ended narrative describing yourself. It's often referred to as the "About Me" section. Wouldn't it be nice if all you had to say were: "Look no further! I will put a smile on your face for the rest of your life, so your search is over: Here I am, just a click away." Well, that is certainly an option! Try it. Sometimes, a novel, outside-the-box approach like this one can yield a fabulous outcome.

Create a Unique Username

IRL (in real life), your username is your smile, your scent, your flirty laugh, your body language, and your gentle touch. IDL (in digital life), your username is your chance to make an unforgettable first impression—and your chance to get her to stop browsing and start clicking on your profile!

So, take your time to select your username—after all, it's the equivalent of your personal brand. It sends a subliminal message about who you are, and it will either attract your ideal match—or make him run faster than a speeding train in the other direction. So your job is to be your very own marketing and public relations manager. And because you only have a nanosecond to grab her interest, creating an intriguing, adorable, unique, fun username is essential. I wish I could give you your own unique username, but since I can't, here are some suggestions to get your creative juices working. Remember, it's all about the two or three words that create an enticing vision of you in his mind's eye—along with your great photos, of course—that'll get him to stop, read, and quickly message you.

Follow my three-part method for designing an unforgettable username:

Part 1: Who are you? Create a list of words that best describe your personality, your characteristics, your "vibe," and your looks. Don't overthink this: Free-associate and come up with a laundry list of adjectives. The more the better—but no fewer than twenty-five, please! Be honest about yourself—but at the same time, focus on your positive qualities. (That shouldn't be hard, since you have so many of them!) See the table on page 13 for examples.

Part 2: Passions and Professions. What are your likes, hobbies, favorite foods? What kind of work do you do? What sort of places do you love? Where are you from, and where do you live now? What are your religious beliefs?

Part 3: The big reveal. Now the fun begins! Once you've compiled your lists, place them next to each other. Now, play a game of mix and match until you've come up with a username that fits you like a glove! Be playful, silly, intriguing—and, of course, flirty. Create a pun; make up a word; and mess around with rhyme. (And check out other people's usernames: They can spark your imagination and give you some great ideas.)

Word to the wise: When brainstorming your lists and creating your username, avoid words that are turn-offs, downers, over the top, tasteless, and downright depressing. Using them will quickly convince potential matches that they don't want or need your shtick, your drama,

HERE'S A LIST OF WORDS NEVER TO INCLUDE IN YOUR USERNAME.

✖ Average	✖ Needy
✖ Bossy	✖ Ordinary
✖ Crazy	✖ Pushy
✖ Drama	✖ Quarrelsome
✖ Envious	✖ Reckless
✖ Fickle	✖ Sad
✖ Gullible	✖ Sexpot
✖ Hot	✖ Tainted
✖ Insecure	✖ Unlucky
✖ Introvert	✖ Vacant
✖ Jaded	✖ Weepy
✖ Kinky	✖ X-rated
✖ Lonely	✖ Yearning
✖ Loner	✖ Zero
✖ Mediocre	

See what I mean? Would you be attracted to 3xdivorced0timeshappy, Pushybroad, Anyguywilldo, or Hototrot? I don't think so.

Also avoid using numbers with your name with a very bland descriptor, like ann22, italian888, or blonde6789.

MIX AND MATCH TRAITS TO CREATE YOUR USERNAME

Describe Yourself	Passions & Professions	Mix & Match
Adorable	Accountant	Love2hustle
Adventurous	Chocolate	Fashionistaupatdawn
Authentic	Coupon queen	Bmytravellove
Brave	Cycling	Persuasivechocoholic
Candid	Dimples	TeckyTreky
Clever	Disco	CulinaryDiva
Compassionate	Disney	Hilariousnightowl
Confident	Editor	ConfidenTriplet
Curious	Fuzzy Navel	PassionatePhD
Devilish	(the cocktail, that is!)	HandsofGold
Empathetic	Gardening	BrightnBold
Entrepreneurial	Ice skating	IrishgaLovesParis
Fashion-forward	Irish	FunnyogaCPA
Fun	IT helpdesk guru	Sweetsushiholic
Funny	Jewelry designer	dimplesngiggles
Generous	Night owl	perfectlyimperfect
Happy	Nurse	resilientsk8ter
Hilarious	Paris	joyfulauthenticRN
Imperfect	Physical therapist	
Insightful	Police officer	
Joyful	Scuba diving	
Kindhearted	Shopaholic	
Lucky	Star Trek	
Nonathletic	Sushi	
Offbeat	Triplet	
Optimistic	X-ray technician	
Outgoing	Yoga	
Passionate		
Persuasive		
Realistic		
Resilient		
Resourceful		
Social butterfly		
Stylish		
Sweet		
Upbeat		

your negativity, or your miserable life. Yes, getting back out there after a breakup is tough: Your heart still hurts at times, but your username is not the place to share your bruises with a stranger. Remember, you are advertising your best and most authentic self—not the hurt, pain, or damage you endured.

Craft a Catchy Headline or Tagline

Your headline is your big chance to make an extraordinary first impression so that he or she will actually want to read your profile. Just like newspapers, headlines sell in the world of online dating, and your goal is to capture his attention instantaneously so he'll read on. Most taglines tend to be mediocre or "blah" with an underlying hint of neediness. Not yours, though! This is your moment—sing your praises, be as clever as you like, show off your wit, or open a window to your soul. Your headline could be a quote with special meaning to you; a line in your favorite song; an expression of something you love; or anything else that tells your dream guy or gal about who you are.

You'll want him to say "wow" when he sees your username and to imagine that you can fill the empty place in his heart. Self-promotion with a touch of humility and tenderness is the ideal blend, as in the examples on the right. I had so much fun coming up with these: Feel free to use any of them!

- City Girl Gone Country
- Denim and Dazzle
- Fabulous and Fit at 40
- Break a Leg
- Leading Lady Seeks Her Love
- Fly Me to the Moon
- U n Me n U So Happy Together
- Seeking Final Puzzle Piece
- Captain Seeks First Mate
- Firecracker Seeks Her Match
- Is Your Heart Open and Ready?
- I'll Turn the Mundane into the Magical
- Lucky, Loving, and Laughter
- Let's Schmooze and See
- Disco Queen Seeks Her King
- Shall We Dance?
- Flexible, Fun, Yoga Gal
- Lifetime Warranty
- I'm a Keeper: Final Sale
- Hairdresser by Day Karaoke by Night
- Let's Start with an Iced Decaf Cappuccino
- Biker Gal
- I Make Great Smiles
- Rx for Love
- When Harry Met Sally
- Lifeguard Always on Duty

Even if your site doesn't require a headline, you should create one anyway.

Put Your Profile Together

You've got your username and headline; now it's time to put together a profile packed with pizzazz. Remember, your profile will take some time and effort, but it doesn't have to be a masterpiece. So hop on your computer, or pick up a notebook or diary, and set aside one to two hours. Go somewhere that puts you in the mood to write—your desk, the library, your favorite coffee shop, or a bookstore café. Once you're comfortable, review the lists you prepared for your username. Consider adding, deleting, or changing them. Sometimes when you revisit your lists, you'll realize you forgot to add important qualities or characteristics that set you apart from others.

Next, complete the following tasks. Be brutally honest, because this exercise is for your eyes only: You will use it as a springboard for writing your (almost) perfect profile.

1. List no more than twelve of your best traits, qualities, and interests. For example:

    - Devoted friend
    - Fabulous Italian cook
    - Loving partner
    - Cross-country skier
    - Fluent in sign language
    - Go-to person for all my friends
    - Party planner
    - Adventurous
    - Mother of amazing twin boys
    - Travel lover

    - Funny
    - Energetic
    - Determined
    - Super-positive

2. Write three short anecdotes of no more than seven lines each that describe who you are by telling an unusual or unique story. In this way, instead of describing yourself—say, as determined and tenacious—you'll "draw a picture" for your potential match. For instance:

How's this for determined?

"I know this is hard to believe but it really is true. (I have the postal receipt to prove it.) I had a defective tire that was two weeks old and no matter what I did, I couldn't get a new tire without incurring a charge. The company finally said, 'The only thing you can do is send it back to us'—and I DID!! Somehow I packed up the tire and got a friend to help me bring it to the post office. The postal worker chuckled and asked us if we were returning the car as well. I asked, 'Do you have a box big enough?'"

Love music and concerts?

"I was so excited to see Adele in concert. When I inquired about where the seats were, the agent said we would be able to see and hear her perfectly. I was thrilled. When we got to the venue, I realized we'd be watching her on the big screen because our seats were in the nosebleed section. Next time I'll look at a seating chart."

You think everyone knows what good-hearted means?

"A few days after 9/11, I was asked if I would join a group of social workers to counsel city workers who had witnessed some horrifying scenes when the towers collapsed. Being there for strangers who were traumatized was heart wrenching yet gratifying. I will never forget how distraught these people were and how fulfilling it was to help."

Get it? After you've written your three anecdotes, edit them and make sure they are succinct and detailed. Read them to a friend or two to get their takes on your stories.

3. List up to twelve qualities, traits, or interests that you're looking for in a mate. For example:

- Affectionate
- Athletic
- History buff
- Introspective
- Marriage-minded
- Non-smoker
- Playful
- Professional
- Sense of humor
- Social
- Vegetarian
- Wants kids

Now you're ready to complete the most labor-intensive part of your profile, which is sometimes referred to as "About Me/ What You Are Looking For."

Review your username, your best traits, your anecdotes, and what you're looking for in a mate, and think about what's most likely to get you noticed. Pick, choose, and write until your profile puts a smile on your face. (By the way, about 75 percent of this section should be about you, and about 25 percent should describe what you are looking for in a partner.)

Here are some tips that'll keep you focused and help you self-promote:

Keep it short and sweet. If you write too much he won't even read it: He'll just skim it at best. So limit this section to no more than 200 words. Think of it this way: You just met someone cute at a party. What would you share about yourself? What questions might you ask? What quirky thing(s) about yourself would you disclose? What do you want him or her to know about you?

Avoid listing what you don't want. Look, I know you want to lay your cards out on the table. You think if you say: no drugs, no cheaters, no liars, no one-night stands, no commitment-phobes, no players, no divorced guys, no one who lives with his parents, no meat-eaters, no one who's self-employed, or no one without a credit card, you've taken out the perfect "insurance policy" against dating disasters. But you're actually doing yourself more harm than good. Sure, maybe some of the casual daters on the site won't message you, but the guys who do meet your specifications will think, "What else about me will she dislike?" And you'll only sound critical, bitter, and impossible to please. So focus on what you do want instead of listing what you don't!

Keep some of your thoughts to yourself. You don't have to spill your guts and divulge everything about yourself in your profile. In fact, full disclosure isn't recommended. Remember, you're promoting yourself, which means shining a spotlight on your accomplishments, talents, and everything wonderful about you. There's no need to tell her you were fired from your most recent job; that you had gastric bypass surgery; that you have some outstanding debt; or how many times your ex cheated on you. And don't dis online dating by saying, "I hate online dating, but my married friend gave me a membership for my birthday." And whatever you do—even if you're thinking it—don't say that online dating is your last resort. Doing so essentially insults anyone who looks at your profile.

Make it conversational. People are drawn to authenticity and sincerity, so you want to make him feel as if you are talking to him. If you can establish an instantaneous connection this way, it's more likely he'll want to message you. Everyone wants to feel safe and secure, and he'll want to be reasonably sure that the gal he reaches out to will be attracted to and drawn toward someone like him. So, in your profile, ask a question like, "Are you ready for the loudest screams when we go on the Rock

N Roller Aerosmith Roller coaster at Disney?" or "Wouldn't it be exciting if we could share our love of Broadway by seeing three shows in one weekend?"

Check your spelling and grammar. Does your spelling or grammar need some polishing? If so, ask a spelling bee champ or grammar-guru friend to check your profile. A 2016 study conducted by Zoosk found that at least 50 percent of men will bypass a profile because of spelling and grammar errors. And 48 percent of the 9,000 singles (both male and female) polled thought that grammar was the biggest online dating deal-breaker. This one's an easy fix—don't overlook it.

Your words speak volumes. According to eHarmony, certain words in straight women's profiles are more attractive to men than others. Here are the best and the worst—but this is just for your information. You decide what feels right for you.

THE BEST
sweet, funny, ambitious, thoughtful, easy going

THE WORST
spiritual, quiet, romantic, good listener, rational

Dating Profiles by the Numbers

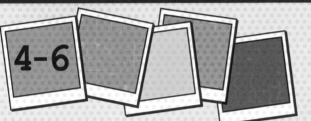

4-6

PHOTOS IN YOUR PROFILE; SEVEN OR MORE IS TOO MANY

12 HOURS

AVERAGE SPENT ON DATING SITES PER WEEK

80%

AMOUNT OF DATING TIME YOU SHOULD SPEND MEETING MATCHES IN PERSON VS ONLINE

$243

AVERAGE SPENT BY DATING SITE CUSTOMER/YEAR

OVER 14 MILLION SINGLES USE DATING APPS

81%

FUDGE THE TRUTH ABOUT THEIR AGE, WEIGHT, AND HEIGHT

49%

SAY PHYSICAL CHARACTERISTICS ARE THE MOST IMPORTANT FACTOR

53%

HAVE DATED MORE THAN ONE PERSON SIMULTANEOUSLY

64%

SAY COMMON INTERESTS ARE THE MOST IMPORTANT FACTOR

» Recent studies can offer some useful suggestions for how to craft the best online dating profile—and common pitfalls to avoid.

Be honest! I can't say this enough. We're all tempted to stretch the truth–but you know what happens on your first date with Mr. or Ms. Right when you've rounded down your age by five years, sliced fifteen-plus pounds off your weight, posted pictures that look nothing like you, or claimed to have two kids when you really have four? I've talked to women who have done this, and here's what a few of them said:

"Within a minute I felt my heart drop to my feet and I just knew he was disappointed."

"It was so awkward and tense. Mr. Potential quickly became Mr. Goodnight."

"As I was driving to the restaurant I was so nervous because I knew I had not been truthful."

Don't let this be you. We all wish we were something we're not: thinner, taller, younger, prettier, more athletic, smarter, richer, bustier, shorter, or gutsier. In fact, according to a *New York Times* article, 81 percent of both men and women fudge the truth about their age, weight, and height. (Women tend to minimize their age and weight. Men tend to maximize their height and occupation.) But when you're honest and truthful in your profile, you're guaranteed that Mr. Potential is looking forward to meeting the *real* you. How wonderful is that?

Writing Your First Flirty Message

I'm not a fan of clichés, and the fact is that good things don't always come to those who wait–especially when it comes to online dating! And if you are truly committed to dating, you need to be ready to make the first move. You can't always wait for the other person to do it. After all, it's up to you to take control of your social life! So get in touch: Send him a flirty email.

Think of your first email as the first course of a great meal. It's the appetizer that whets your appetite for the main course– which is meeting in person, of course. With that in mind, I think it's best to be forward and direct in your first email. (Don't worry: I'm not suggesting you schedule your first date at the Macy's bridal registry!) Think of your email as a puzzle in which all of the pieces need to fit together.

Puzzle Piece #1: Craft a connection. The main purpose of your email is to establish a bond with a stranger. You want her to feel at ease with you.

Puzzle Piece #2. Make sure you have read his profile. Comment about something he wrote, or ask a question to get the conversation flowing. You could say, "I am so impressed that you went to Iceland for a quick getaway by yourself! I would love to hear about your adventure. I went to an all-inclusive beach resort on my own, and I thought that was gutsy—but not nearly as brave as your trip."

Puzzle Piece #3: Give compliments with class. Don't you feel absolutely amazing when you receive a wonderful compliment? Self-doubt melts away, and you feel like you're on top of the world. The same is true for her—which is why paying a compliment is the perfect way to let her know you are a class act. Here's how to do it with style:

- Dish out two compliments in your initial email: one on his appearance and one on his character: "*You have the best hair. I am so jealous.*" "*I was very impressed how you described what's important to you in a relationship. I said to myself, this is the kind of guy I would love to meet.*"

- The best compliments are sincere, genuine, and out of the ordinary. Be sure that yours fit this description. "*I appreciated the time and effort you put into writing the most interesting and intriguing profile I have ever seen. It captured my attention, and my heart!*" "*You have the greatest legs, the cutest smile, and your profile is pretty amazing, too!*"

- No left-handed compliments. They can make you seem sarcastic and insincere. *What's a successful guy like you doing on an online dating site?*"

Puzzle Piece #4: Use every opportunity to grab his attention. The goal of digital flirting is threefold: make him smile, pique his interest, and show you are attracted to him. And luckily, you have three separate opportunities in every email to do just that. Here they are:

SUBJECT LINE

We all get lots of emails each day. The ones I open first are those with an inviting subject line. So flaunt your flirty side right from the start:

Boring subject lines sound like, "Hi from Fran," "Good evening," or "Pleasant profile."

Inviting subject lines sound like, "Who knows? I could be the one." "Guaranteed to make you smile." "We both have labradoodles, they'll have to meet!" "How fantastic that we both love the beach in the winter."

SALUTATION

You only get one chance to make an unforgettable first impression! So, capture her attention from the moment you say hello.

Run-of-the-mill salutations sound like, "Hello," "Greetings," or "How are you?"

Attention-grabbing salutations sound like, "Dear Delicious Chocoholic" (if, for instance, she talked about being a chocolate lover), "So glad to meet you," "Dear Baby Blue Eyes" (only if she has blue eyes, of course!), or "Thanks for posting your profile."

CLOSING

Your closing is so important. You want him to feel that he is the only guy you want to meet. Once he senses that you're into him, he will feel super-confident contacting you because you made him feel desired.

Mind-numbing closings sound like, "Have a good day," "Yours truly," "Take care," or, worst of all, no closing and just signing your name.

Intriguing closings sound like, "Wouldn't it be great if I were your last first date?" "Hearing your voice would be the icing on the cake," "Meeting you would be awesome," "It would be so much fun to continue our conversation in person," or "Today is my lucky day: I saw your profile."

Puzzle Piece #5: Add a question. That'll give you more insight into him/her. One of my favorites is, "If money were no object, what would you do for a living?" The answer might be a perfect springboard for a conversation when you meet.

Puzzle Piece #6: Tell him you'd like to talk. Here, you're saving the best for last! Let him know you would like to discuss meeting. "Your profile was so real and down to earth, and the story about 'losing your car' in the airport parking lot was hysterical. (I did the same thing at a shopping mall: I ran around looking for the security office and told them my car had been stolen—only to realize I went out a different exit.) If you're interested, let's talk on the phone and see where it goes. Looking forward to hearing from you sooner than later. P.S.: Your photo was the icing on the cake. Warmly, Janelle"

By the way, I recommend waiting no more than one or two days to make a plan to meet once you've started to communicate. (The meeting doesn't have to happen immediately, but the plan for it does.) As exciting as all of your emails and texts seem, none of it matters if you don't meet in person.

Safety First

Okay, so you've winked at him, liked his photo, checked "yes" to wanting to meet him, emailed, texted, and talked on the phone. The chemistry is great and you are so excited to meet. And the best part is that you feel as if you've known him your whole life.

I get it! After being "dateless" for so long, it feels amazing to be this excited about going on a date. You feel wanted, attractive, and worthy. You never thought you would get to that place—and here you are. Congratulations! But I'm not surprised. I knew you would get there. You have, and you earned it.

Stay Safe: What NOT to Do

Now, I don't mean to be a downer, but I care about you and want you to think with your head and not your heart when it comes to being safety savvy. Smart women can make—and have made—foolish decisions when it comes to navigating online dating. So, if you are new to online dating, or are getting back into it after a breakup, remind yourself that safety always comes first. Always remember the following: He is a stranger, no matter how great the vibes between you are.

Here are some examples of what *not to do* under any circumstances on a first date with an online match:

✖ Lindsey and Adam exchanged several emails. She lived in the suburbs and he lived in the city. They arranged for him to take the train to her town. She would pick him up at the train station and drive him to the restaurant. *Do not get into a car together.*

✖ Alyssa was driving to the city to meet Brian. Since parking was a nightmare, he suggested that she come to his house and park in his driveway, have a drink at his house, and then walk to the restaurant. *Do not go to his house.*

✖ Debbie was on cloud nine because Bruce was everything she was looking for in a man. So, for their first date, she invited him to pick her up at her home in his car, and then head to dinner together. *Do not ask him to come to your house; do not get into his car.*

✖ Melissa was enamored of Jake. He lived in New Jersey and she lived in Philadelphia. He suggested they meet in Atlantic City, go to the casino, and stay overnight. The next morning, he told her he was putting his bag in his car and never returned. *Do not stay overnight together.*

Stay Safe: What TO Do

That's my list of don'ts. So here's what you *should* do to stay safe—no matter how much you like him or how thrilled you are at the prospect of dating again.

Use an unidentifiable email. If your email address is your first and last name—for example, JaneDoe@fakemail.com—don't use it for your online dating matches. Sign up for a free account at Gmail, Yahoo, or Hotmail instead. Your online dating email should not include any personal data, like your full name, age, address, or the town in which you live. Try an address like "lovetohustle@gmail.com," "msfixit@yahoo.com," or "poodlelvr@hotmail.com." This is essential when you transition from the anonymous email feature provided through the dating site to your private email. Remember, your personal email address is a link to a whole host of additional information on the Internet and should not be immediately shared.

Shhh, it's a secret. Never include any of the following in your username, profile, or in your first email to your potential date:

- Your first and last name
- Your home address
- Your cell, work, or home phone numbers
- Where you work
- Your email address
- Your date of birth
- Any other personal or identifying information

You don't want your date to know your private info until you are comfortable with him. As the saying goes, an ounce of prevention is worth a pound of cure. (Of course, you'll certainly exchange cell phone numbers if you decide you want to text each other and to make plans to meet.)

Always meet in a public place. Choose a place that is comfortable and familiar: You'll automatically feel more at ease. Make sure that the place you select is busy and has plenty of parking (or can be reached easily by public transportation). Coffee shops, restaurants, bookstores, sports bars, and pubs are all great "public" spots to meet. And not only should you meet in a public place, but the entire date should also take place in a setting with lots of other people around. Stay away from a secluded park or beach or any location off the beaten path.

Get yourself to and from the date. Always provide your own transportation to your first meeting. Never get picked up at your home or office or at a friend's place. And no matter how well the date went, always, *always* get yourself home on your own!

Make sure your cell phone is charged. Always have your cell phone with you, and make sure it's fully charged. And have a contact plan: Many women arrange to text or call a friend at a specific time during the course of the date to confirm that everything is okay. You can excuse yourself and duck into the ladies' room to call or text your friend, and your date doesn't have to know you're doing it. I also encourage my clients to text a friend when they get home from the date.

Share your itinerary. Let your friend, neighbor, or relative know where you are going, who you are going with, and when you expect to be home. Text this information to your contact person or leave the info on your kitchen table.

Stick to the one-drink rule. No matter how much you love those watermelon martinis, never have more than one drink. Alcohol has a funny way of making us lose our inhibitions—and our good judgment.

It's okay to change your mind. Please, always remember this: You never have to feel obligated to go through with a date. If your gut instinct tells you not to go, then cancel your plans. Be polite yet firm. Also, if you arrive at the date and it doesn't feel right for any reason, make any excuse you want and then leave. You could say that you are feeling really sick to your stomach and you don't want to embarrass him. (Well, it's sort of the truth.)

Use common sense . . . Online dating sites want their members to feel safe and they're committed to doing what they can to provide you with a positive experience. But, although some sites claim to do background checks, most don't—and

DO A LITTLE DIGITAL SLEUTHING

Your date may willingly share his email address, last name, and/or phone number. If you have them, it's a good idea to check him out by doing a quick Internet search. Here are some of the things to be on the lookout for:

- Is what he told you about himself consistent with the info you found? (If not, why is he lying?)

- Did his photo come from a stock photo site? (If so, he might be a scammer.)

- Is where he lives different then what he told you? (Why the discrepancy?)

- Is his work information contradictory to what he told you? (What is he hiding?)

- Does he appear with another woman in all of his Facebook photos? (Perhaps he already has a girlfriend.)

- Did you find his name in the local paper's police blotter? (If so, he may be trouble.)

If what he has told you and what you've found in your search don't match, don't ignore it. It might be best to move on to someone who is upfront, truthful, and has nothing to hide.

even if they do, it'll only provide you with a false sense of security. The best security measure is your common sense and your intuition.

. . . and your sixth sense. Call it your gut feeling, your inner voice, woman's intuition, or whatever you like—just listen to it. If your match is pushy, controlling, argumentative, pressures you, sends inappropriate photos or messages, or bullies you during any of your communication, cease all contact immediately. Don't waste another second on this loser, and report any harassment or inappropriate behavior to the dating site.

Keep an eye on your drink. Please don't leave your drink unattended. We've all heard horror stories about drugs being slipped into drinks—it's always better to be cautious.

Beware of scammers. Thankfully, this one's pretty rare. Still, here are some red flags that scream SCAM:

- He asks you for money, your credit card number, bank account details, or asks you to wire him money.

> Trust your sixth sense—it's the best way to stay safe. If it feels creepy or just not right, DO NOT ignore your feelings.

- He is in another country but needs help getting back to your country.

- He never wants to meet in person.

- He wants your address to send you flowers or a gift.

- He gives you a sob story about needing money for a blood transfusion for his very ill child or tells you his sick mother needs expensive medications.

- He expresses his love for you after one or two contacts.

- He sends links to other websites, especially pornographic sites.

- He never answers any of your questions, contradicts himself, and always has an emergency.

If you have any concerns, contact the website immediately and block all contact from the suspicious person.

Dating Apps

Dating apps usually have a fun, light-hearted vibe. Their very names make you want to get into the game and play—like Bumble, Tinder, Coffee Meets Bagel, and Hinge. Of course, there are niche apps as well, such as Bristlr (for beard lovers); the League (for Ivy League grad-types); and Taste Buds, which matches you according to your taste in music. These apps aim to make your love life simple and uncomplicated. That's fine, but never completely throw caution to the wind. As with dating sites, safety always comes first, so be sure to follow the safety guidelines I outlined on page 127.

Apps are efficient; you don't have to write much about who you are or what you're looking for. In keeping with apps' brevity, here's a quick rundown of what makes them so popular:

- Most apps are free.
- Many online dating sites include a mobile app.
- Apps are accessible wherever you go.
- Some apps require that you have a Facebook account to sign in.
- They're easy to use; most require only a sentence or two plus a photo.
- You can see if you have any friends in common.
- Many apps connect you with others in your vicinity while you are logged in.

- Apps reward instantaneous action. On Tinder, for example, you swipe right when you like a potential match. If he swipes right on your profile, too, you have a match! But once you swipe left once, he's gone, so you have to be decisive.
- Apps let you down easy: You'll never know who has left-swiped you! This is a great feature, especially if rejection makes you cringe.
- Some sites send you only one match per day: That's good if you tend to feel overwhelmed by too many potential matches.
- Most apps don't have the functionality to search for specific criteria, like a blonde who likes horseback riding.
- Apps mirror texting, making them a quick and easy way to search for a match.
- Some people use apps for casual hookups—but not all of them.
- Over 14 million singles are using apps.
- Apps are a fun new twist on the "old" concept of online dating sites.
- You'll need to be patient as you wade through all the smiling faces.

As with dating sites, I suggest trying one mainstream app and one niche app to get a sense of what apps have to offer.

Going on a Date

Transitioning from an On-Screen Romance to a Real-Life Love Affair

There's nothing more important than meeting in person, and nothing can take the place of meeting face to face. Again, plan to meet within a couple of days of making contact, otherwise there's a greater chance you'll be disappointed. As your onscreen love affair grows, you also develop what I call "pseudo-intimacy"– or, to put it simply, make-believe. Your expectations are exploding all around you, and you're idealizing him so much that it's highly unlikely he'll match up to your hopes and dreams. Don't give this pseudo-intimacy time to develop. Instead, meet in person to see if there's real-life chemistry between you.

Everyone dates a little differently, and while there are no set rules for how a first date should be arranged, here are some pitfalls to avoid while you're making plans for date number one:

- **Avoid an email love affair.** It's best to have only a few back-and-forth emails before you meet. Even just one or two is fine. Remember, the purpose of exchanging emails is to decide whether you want to meet.

- **Avoid becoming IMing pals.** Don't IM for more than a day or two at most. As with email, the purpose of instant messaging is to decide if you want to meet in person.

- **Avoid having a relationship via text.** Text back and forth for no more than a day or two. Again, at this point, the purpose of texting is to decide whether the two of you will meet.

- **Avoid talking on the phone for more than fifteen minutes.** It's possible to "fall in love with" a person's voice, only to be totally disappointed when you meet in person.

- **Don't wait too long to make a date.** Make a date to get together within one week of your initial contact–even if the date is scheduled for more than a week away.

If he still just wants to be your virtual date, tell him you are not available via technology: You are only available for an in-person chat. If he doesn't get it, just tell him you aren't interested and send him on his virtual way.

But what if you meet Mr. Right, and he turns out to be Mr. Wrong? In that case, be gently honest with him about how you feel. Don't chicken out and "ghost" him instead. "Ghosting" means disappearing into thin air–no calls, no messages–after a date. Some daters see it as the default setting if you're not interested, but not me. If you aren't feeling it, say so and let him know in the kindest way possible that date number two isn't in the stars. (Yes, you can wait until he asks you out for the next date to tell him.) This is the right thing to do because this way he won't be kept guessing. (You know what that feels like!) You can say it in person, on the phone, via text, or via email. For suggestions for tactful ways to say you're not interested, see page 72.

The Emotional Perils of Online Dating

Dating again after a breakup is a double-edged sword. You want to get back out there and feel like your old self again—with confidence, a happy heart, and hope for the future. But dating can resurrect those locked-away feelings of insecurity, doom, and gloom. Never fear: I'm going to take you through some potential hazards of online dating—and show you how to minimize the effects of each. This way, you can reframe your attitude and look forward to the whole process of this new adventure—even when obstacles crop up.

EXHAUSTION

The whole process of online dating can be emotionally draining. After all, whenever you put your heart on the line, you use up a ton of psychic energy. If you find yourself feeling exhausted, take an online dating vacation. For how long? You decide—a day, a week, a month. The goal is to give your heart a rest, in the same way you give your body a rest after a long, hard workout. Take the shortest vacation possible while still giving yourself time to recover. If you take too much time off, it can be hard to work up the strength to get back into it.

YOU FEEL LIKE A KID IN A CANDY SHOP

Online dating can be overwhelming and exhilarating at the same time. It isn't unusual to feel consumed with and fascinated by your search. Some women have told me that they're obsessed with the never-ending pursuit of a profile that's better than the one that came before it. All this means that it's so easy to become overly picky and judgmental. Sometimes your narrow checklist rules out a great guy who'd be a good match. We often think we know exactly what we want based on a profile—even though a person's potential for being a great partner isn't based on his or her favorite TV shows or political persuasion. The bottom line is that we overvalue stuff that, ultimately, has little to do with true happiness. The only way to know if she or he is right is to meet IRL.

YOU'RE EXCLUSIVELY DATING ONLINE

Online dating can be your go-to dating mode, but not to the exclusion of the other dating options we've talked about. Remember, you can also go on blind dates; to singles' events; meet people through work, hobbies, or volunteering; or by getting your real-life flirt on in ways I recommended in Step 3 (see page 79). So, give yourself a time limit when it comes to looking for your next online date(s).

On weekdays, this limit may be no more than one hour a day, or two hours on the weekends. Otherwise, it's way too easy to spend hours on end sifting through profile after profile, hoping the next one will be "better" than the last. So, follow the 80/20 rule: Spend 80 percent of your dating time making connections in real life, and 20 percent doing the online stuff—browsing, flirting, IMing, emailing, texting, and talking on the phone. "Dating online" is an oxymoron; you "meet" someone online before you have a date in person!

YOU'VE GOT TUNNEL VISION

This is a tricky one. All right: You signed on to online dating to find your perfect match. That's the beauty (and the beast!) of online dating. We all end up convincing ourselves that if he lives ten miles away, is

> Follow the 80/20 rule: Spend 80 percent of your dating time making connections in real life, and 20 percent pursuing dates online.

three years your senior, loves to cook, and his favorite music is country, he'll be absolutely perfect and the two of you will sail off into the sunset together. This can and does happen, but for most of us mortals, all of the matching criteria in the world will never replace the way you click with him. So cast your net just a bit wider by increasing your mileage requirements, changing your height specs, or widening your age range. He just might live forty miles away, love jazz, and sweep you off your feet on your first date. At the end of the day, it's all about how you feel when you're together.

Online Dating Rocks

Although online dating can be grueling, it can be equally exhilarating. Anyone who has been in its trenches knows this firsthand—and anyone who has met the love of her life in this way is forever grateful for putting herself out there. Be sure to approach online dating with optimism and humor—the same way your approach real-life flirting. It's the best way to stay positive, focused, and driven.

TIPS FOR GREAT DATES

Here's how to make your online dating adventure as fun and fulfilling as possible:

- Have first dates with lots of different people.

- Choose to have a positive attitude! It keeps you going when your last date was so boring that you wished you'd stayed at home cleaning out your sock drawer.

- Don't get swayed by sites with huge numbers of users. Bigger isn't always better.

- Instant success is fabulous, not the norm. Be prepared to be patient.

- Be proactive. Don't sit back and wait for your next match to pick you! Send a wink, like his photo, and—better yet—take a deep breath and send her an inviting email.

- Safety first, fun second. Revisit the safety tips in this step (see page 127) and stick to them.

- The best antidote to a disappointing date? Having the next date lined up!

- Thank yourself for investing your heart, soul, and time into this process. You're worth it.

A dream written down with a date becomes a goal. A goal broken down into steps becomes a plan. A plan backed by action makes your dreams come true.

—GREG S. REID,
WWW.THESILVERPEN.COM

Step 5

EMBRACE YOUR FUTURE: Embark on Your Personal 60-Day Dating Action Plan

Fasten your seat belt! This detailed, 60-day dating action plan will help you dive into the dating pool. Building on and reinforcing all of the previous steps in this book, your 60-day plan will focus on your individual dating goal—whether that's casual dating, a long-term relationship, or even marriage. The plan will help you break your goal into smaller, more doable pieces, making it easier to visualize and more achievable.

Dating is a skill, and, just as with any other skill, repetition, review, and revision are all necessary for improving it—and for reaching your goal. So, if anything sounds familiar to you in this chapter, it's for a reason: It's really important—even vital—to hear it again. Besides, after a breakup, you might not be ready to absorb the information quickly (and shifts in attitude) that you need to get your dating life back up and running. That's okay: Take your time and sit with it. It'll sink in. I promise.

So now it's time to embrace your future and get back out there with the hopeful and optimistic attitude you've cultivated. Embrace the mindset that love is possible. Yes, there will be ups and downs and some minor disappointments along the way, but not to worry: You can handle it. I promise! Your increased self-confidence, coupled with lots of new dating

opportunities (that you create) will be the hallmarks of your success.

Here's what to expect in the coming weeks. By the end of your 60-Day Dating Challenge, you will:

- Be a confident and resilient dater
- Flirt naturally and effortlessly
- Be an online dating connoisseur
- Act as your own dating service
- Let go of your ex so you can bring new love into your life
- Look forward to attending singles' events and other social gatherings
- Have a fabulous online dating profile
- Take control of your love and social life
- Never let a dating opportunity pass you by

 # *The Spirit of Resilience*

Resilience is your best attribute as you move forward with your 60-day action plan. But being resilient doesn't mean you'll never encounter a creepy guy, a boring evening, some form of rejection, or an event that's uncomfortable or stressful. What it means is this: Resilient daters bounce back. They don't allow rejection to consume them or let a really horrible singles' event predict the outcome of every event in the future. Instead, they—

and you!—view adversity, fear, self-doubt, and worries about the future as a reminder to persevere and to reflect on a positive aspect of whatever they encounter. You know that a hopeful, positive perspective is key to success. And the more resilient you are, the easier it is to look forward to the next adventure on your dating expedition. Ultimately, resilience builds strength and promotes happiness.

Start with Your Destination

Dating and finding love requires action—yours! It doesn't happen by chance. I know there are a handful of women out there who got super-lucky after their divorce or breakup. Perhaps they got into a fender-bender and wound up living happily ever after with Mr. Happy Accident. Or maybe your best friend got fixed up with a recent widower and hasn't looked back. That's great, but chance encounters like these rarely happen. So don't wait around for Mr. Wonderful to magically appear.

Instead, I'm putting the power in your hands by helping you set a goal—the best way to convert a dating dream into tangible results. This is also true in the world of business: When entrepreneurs set quantifiable goals, they are more likely to get results. So think of yourself as a dating entrepreneur—someone willing to make an investment to reap long-term gains.

Your Personal Dating Action Plan

Each daily or weekly assignment is designed to help you take the plunge. There is no tiptoeing into this swimming pool—if you do, you'll never get in! Instead, dive into dating with a splash—and feel exhilarated and excited while doing it.

During the sixty days, you will:

- ✔ Go on eight first dates
- ✔ Attend one singles' event alone
- ✔ Attend two singles' events with a friend
- ✔ Attend one non-singles' activity
- ✔ Attend two social events
- ✔ Attend two speed-dating events
- ✔ Attend two singles' meetup groups
- ✔ Attend one non-singles' meetup group
- ✔ Sign up for one mainstream dating site
- ✔ Sign up for one niche dating site
- ✔ Sign up for one mobile dating app
- ✔ Spend seven hours per week browsing dating sites
- ✔ Send one to five emails per day on your mainstream dating site

- ✔ Send one to three emails per day on your niche dating site
- ✔ Swipe right on seven to ten people per day
- ✔ Smile at and make eye contact with strangers
- ✔ Start conversations with strangers

OPTIONAL
- ✔ Exchange phone numbers with a prospective date you meet in real life
- ✔ Ask out one person you meet in real life
- ✔ Journal your feelings and thoughts

This might sound like a lot at first, but don't worry! My goal—and yours—is for you to complete your 60-Day Dating Challenge successfully, happily, and with an amazing feeling of accomplishment. And here's how we're going to do it.

Your Weekly Snapshot

At the beginning of each week, you'll get a "snapshot" of the week ahead as an overview of what you can expect to accomplish. It's designed to help you plan your schedule and get excited.

Your Weekly Assignment

Each week, you'll attend an activity or go on a date on a day of your choosing. Just make sure that you schedule it on your calendar and mark it as completed. If life gets in the way, that's okay: Reschedule, re-mark your calendar, and note the "completed" date in your calendar.

Your Daily To-Do List

This section includes all of the tasks you will complete by the end of the day in question. As the weeks pass, your daily to-do list will encompass several days rather than just focus on a single day at a time. (At the beginning of each week, it's best to review your assignments for the coming days: This will help you manage your time efficiently and effectively.)

You're in the Driver's Seat

You set the pace during the sixty days to come. If you want to move faster, that's fine: Feel free to move ahead to the next day's assignments. Slowing down for a bit is okay too: It's all up to you. Just keep in mind that you do want to reach your goal at the end of your 60-Day Dating Challenge.

Your Personal Dating Trainer

This is someone who will keep you moving and motivated and isn't afraid to tell it like it is. Select a good friend (single or married); man or woman (straight or gay); family member (sibling, cousin); or a dating coach. Your personal dating trainer will make sure you stay on track.

Social Events

I know that going to or hosting a social event isn't always easy after a breakup or divorce. But it's still important to accept social invitations and to make social plans.

During your 60-Day Dating Challenge, you'll attend two social events. You might want to attend or host:

- Parties
- Dinners with friends
- A happy hour with colleagues
- Weddings, sweet sixteens, or christenings
- Holiday get-togethers

Singles' Events

You'll attend three singles' events during the sixty days. A singles' event is simply an organized event in which all attendees are single. It could be a flirting/dating workshop followed by mingling and socializing; a walk on the boardwalk plus lunch in a restaurant; or it could be a discussion group focused on a topic of particular interest to singles, like being single parents and dating, or the pros and cons of dating more than one person at a time.

Events like these are great places to make new friends, meet someone to date, and engage in an activity with other people who have also experienced a breakup.

To find events in your area, check:

- Your local newspaper
- Adult education courses geared toward singles
- Religious institutions that have events, services, and groups for singles
- Community centers
- Town- or city-sponsored events
- Nearby colleges and universities, which may feature classes and events for singles
- Events sponsored by online dating sites—these are fun, unique, and are for members only

If there are no singles' events in your area, don't give up: Consider traveling an hour or two to go to one.

Speed Dating

Yes, you're going to try this! During your 60-Day Dating Challenge, you'll attend two speed-dating events. Here's what to expect:

At each speed-dating event, there are equal numbers of men and women in the same age range—usually no more than thirty in total. At the start of the event, each participant puts on a name tag with his or her first name and a number. She or he is also equipped with a scorecard. When the event kicks off, everyone partners up. One man and one woman (if it's a straight event) sit down at an individual table and have five minutes to get to know each other and to decide whether they want to see each other again.

At the end of the five-minute "date," each person marks "yes" or "no" on the scorecard: It's a "yes" if you want to go out on a date with the other person, and it's a "no" if you don't. As the event continues, either the men or women move from table to table until everyone has gotten a chance to meet. It's a lot of fun!

Because you're meeting lots of new people all at once, it's a good idea to have a few questions on hand in case the conversation needs a boost. Here are some fun ones:

- What age do you wish you were and why?
- What kitchen utensil best describes you and why?
- Tell me anything and everything about your name.
- What is your most treasured possession and why?
- What is your favorite fast food or junk food?

- Tell me about your first childhood pet.
- If you had three wishes, what would they be?
- If you could be any vegetable, which one would you be?

After the event, the organizers compile the findings. If two people have a mutual "YES," it's a match! Then the organizers email the mutual matches with first names and email addresses. It's up to you to decide if you want to contact your match.

Speed dating is an interactive and efficient way to meet about twelve people in a single evening. And since your "thumbs-up" or "thumbs-down" rating is anonymous, you can leave the event with the happy anticipation that you'll have made a few connections. Do an Internet search for "speed-dating events in [your area]" to find one near you. (And if you really can't find a speed-dating event in your area on your designated day, that's okay: Substitute another singles' event for it.)

Name	Yes	No	Maybe	Notes
Mike			✓	Teacher, beard
Dustin	☺			Funny!
William		✗		
Lucas	✓			Nice eyes
Rod		✓		
Pedro			✓	Cute but too serious?

» Here's an example of what a speed-dating scorecard could look like.

Non-Singles' Activity

A non-singles' activity is any leisure event that involves interaction with other people. Be as friendly as possible and be ready to make small talk as you enjoy the event. The options are endless, but here are some examples:

- Take a class (yoga, art, wine tasting)
- Go to an outdoor festival
- Attend a sporting event
- Visit a museum
- Join a book club (at your local library, a bookstore, or a coffee shop)
- Check out an art exhibit
- Go to quiz or trivia night at your local bar
- Volunteer for a cause you support (homeless shelter, animal rescue)

Meetup Groups

Meetup groups are another great way to connect with people. Check out meetup.com to find one in your area. It claims to be the world's largest network of local groups, with more than 27 million members attending 250,000 meetup groups in 180 countries. During your 60-Day Dating Challenge, you'll attend one non-singles' meetup group and two singles' meetup groups. Groups are based on common interests and experiences, such as divorce, breakup, single parents, careers, book clubs, fitness, arts and culture, hobbies and crafts, environment, health and well-being, sports, technology, food, and many others. (P.S.: If the speed-dating event, meetup group, or singles' event you'd like to attend doesn't take place during the specified week, that's fine: Go to it on the date it's scheduled.)

Optional Extras

Here are a few things you can add to your 60-Day Dating Challenge. Think of them as a bonus. The more you do, the better you'll feel and the closer you'll get to finding the relationship you truly want.

- **Exchange phone numbers with a prospective date you meet in real life**. Imagine this: You're out and about doing your thing, and, when you least expect it, you meet someone who's single and available and you kind of like her. You start talking and you find yourself thinking, "Wow, I'm interested her!" Take a

SMALL TALK

No matter where you are or what you're doing during your 60-Day Dating Challenge, you'll strike up lots of conversations with people you don't know. If this makes you feel nervous, don't worry: Practice is the best antidote for nerves! So practice with women, men, kids, someone older than you, someone younger than you, a guy that you think is cute, or someone who looks like they would appreciate a few friendly words. Back in kindergarten, not talking to strangers was a safety precaution. These days, doing the opposite and talking to lots of strangers is a great way to make connections. You never know where a conversation might lead!

deep breath and tell yourself that if you do nothing you get nothing—and then go for it. Smile and say with confidence, "How about we exchange phone numbers?" Then hand her your card. You did it! Even if she doesn't call you—or if you don't call her—you seized the moment and took the risk. Congratulations!

- **Ask someone out whom you've already met in person**. You've meet someone who really grabs your attention. Maybe you've seen him several times and are getting good vibes, but he hasn't asked you out. Well, remember our talk about chutzpah and charm (see page 86)? Here's where they come into play! Matter-of-factly, but with enthusiasm, just ask him out. You could say, "Are you up for dinner tomorrow night?" "Would you like to go for an early walk and breakfast on Sunday?" or "I have tickets for a concert: Would you be interested in going?" Just do it.

- **Journal your thoughts and feelings in your 60-Day Dating Challenge notebook**. Grab your notebook and jot down a thought or feeling that comes up for you each day of your Challenge. You don't have to write a novel—a sentence or two will do. You'll find this helpful later, because you'll be able to see how you felt and what you were thinking as you moved through the process—and how far you've come.

We're all human, so during your Challenge, there will be days when you won't be in the mood, or are just tired or cranky. On those days, give yourself an extra push and ask your personal dating trainer for some encouragement. Or, think of me—since I'm acting as your dating coach right now!—and say to yourself, "Fran knows I can do it and she is my biggest cheerleader. She wants me to succeed." When you feel better, you'll see that all you needed was a little reassurance and inspiration.

Let's get started with Week #1!

STUCK FOR OPENING LINES?

Here are a few easy ways to start a conversation with new people:

Talk about the surroundings. Be spontaneous and light-hearted when you make your approach. "Wow, what a pleasure—no line at the checkout!" "This place has the best thin-crust pizza." "This is the cleanest gym I have ever seen." "It's so beautiful out today, especially after all that humidity we've been having."

Ask an open-ended question. Open-ended questions require more than a "yes" or "no" answer and are a great way to break the ice. "Any drink recommendations? I never know which one to get." "Do you know where the closest gas station is?" "There are so many burgers on the menu: Which are your favorites?" "I've never made quinoa: Which brand do you like?"

Give a compliment. "You have the best hair!" "I love your shoes, where did you get them?" "What an adorable baby. What's her name?" "I love your necklace." "Your bicycle is amazing."

Just say "Hi" with a smile. Simple, low-key, and effective!

Week 1

WEEK #1 IS ABOUT:

- Identifying your goals
- Establishing your online dating presence
- Introducing yourself to available people
- Selecting your personal dating trainer

THIS WEEK YOU WILL:

✔ Attend one social event

✔ Attend one singles' event alone

✔ Check in with your dating trainer

Day 1

Welcome to Day 1 of your 60-Day Dating Challenge! Today, you will complete the following tasks:

✔ Mark your calendar.

✔ Check off your goals.

✔ List your top two goals.

✔ List your top five deal breakers.

✔ List your top five must-haves.

IF IT'S NOT ON THE CALENDAR, IT'S ONLY A WISH

The 60-Day Dating Challenge is about making wishes come true. So use the planner provided on page 154, open your Google calendar or get one to hang on the wall or place on your desk, and label today as Day 1. Then number each consecutive day until you reach Day 60. It's important to see how close Day 60 really is. (It'll be here before you even blink!)

As you'll see, each day's schedule builds on the previous day's, while preparing you for what's ahead. But you have a busy life filled with responsibilities, to-do lists, and deadlines, plus the unknown—like a surprise visit from an out-of-town guest, a work event, or (heaven forbid!) a case of the measles! So you'll want to plan in advance as much as possible to make sure you reach your goals. Don't skip this step: If it's not on your calendar, it won't happen!

WHAT IS YOUR ULTIMATE GOAL?

Now is the time to set your goal for the future. (This is where you actually make your dream come true.) Your goal is the outcome you want to achieve as the result of this process. It will give you direction and focus for the next sixty days.

Take a look at the following list and check off any (or all) that apply to you.

What are you looking for?

˙ Meeting new people

˙ Meeting new people to date

˙ Having three or more dates with one person

˙ Having six or more dates with one person

˙ A serious or committed relationship

˙ Living together in a committed relationship

˙ Marriage

DEFINING YOUR GOALS

Jenna, a woman I interviewed, was dumped without warning by her boyfriend of two years. It had been three months since her breakup, and she was ready to be more mindful and proactive about dating. She felt she had been dating *without* a purpose, but now wanted to focus and come up with a plan. Jenna said, with a laugh, "I just want to date more." When I asked what she was looking for, she said thoughtfully, "I am looking for someone I can really connect with; someone who makes me a priority in his life, and vice versa. Who knows where it might lead?" Then Jenna was able to select her top two goals: Meeting new people to date and having three or more dates with one person.

Great. Now, pick your top two goals—the ones you want to achieve within the next sixty days. I want you to push yourself just enough so that you feel a little stretched—while feeling at the same time that your goal is attainable. Attainability is important: I want you to feel triumphant on each and every day of your dating challenge.

#1 Goal _____

#2 Goal _____

Perfect! You have selected your top two goals for the next sixty days and you have a direction and a destination. (And even though you've selected your goals now, you're not "married"—pardon the pun!—to your selection. You can revise your goals at any time during your 60-Day Challenge.)

YOUR MUST-HAVES

Knowing what you need in a partner is so important. Here are some common must-haves.

- Ambitious
- Curious
- Family-oriented
- Interesting and interested
- Makes me a priority in his or her life
- Open-minded
- Seeks an equal partner
- Sense of adventure
- Sense of humor
- Values my time with my kids
- Wants kids/doesn't want kids
- Wants marriage/doesn't want marriage
- Wants to travel
- Well-groomed

Think about what you need to be happy, and think about what you didn't have in your previous relationship(s). Reflect back on what you wished you had: You know, the things you minimized in your mind at the time but always knew deep down that you'd never be happy without them. These are the qualities, behaviors, life goals—and, maybe, a couple of idiosyncratic things—that you truly need and want in your next loving relationship. List as few or as many as you'd like:

_____

_____

_____

_____

_____

_____

_____

_____

Now that you know what you want in a partner, let's identify your deal breakers. This way you won't waste time on someone clearly not right for you. Here are some common deal breakers:

- Antisocial
- Controlling
- Detached
- Wants/doesn't want kids
- Wants/doesn't want marriage
- Drug use
- Lazy
- Macho
- No sense of humor
- Pompous or arrogant
- Problems with an ex
- Selfish
- Smoker
- Unkempt appearance, poor hygiene

Of course, these are just ideas. Your personal deal breakers are unique to you. List them in the space below. List as few or as many behaviors, lifestyle choices, personality traits, or interests that you just can't live with.

_____

_____

_____

_____

_____

_____

_____

Days 2 and 3

- ✔ Read a friend's dating profile.
- ✔ Ask two friends to text you five words that best describe you.
- ✔ Ask two friends to share a funny memory of you.
- ✔ Ask two friends to send you their favorite photos of you.
- ✔ Choose a username.
- ✔ Select a headline.
- ✔ Create your profile: "About Me" and what you are looking for.
- ✔ Celebrate your accomplishment!

READ A FRIEND'S ONLINE DATING PROFILE

Before you begin work on your profile, ask a friend to share his or hers with you. It's a great way to get those creative juices flowing.

A LITTLE HELP FROM YOUR FRIENDS

There's no need to go it alone! Ask your friends for help. Get two of them to text or email you the following things:

- Five words that best describe you
- A funny memory of you
- A favorite photo of you

> **Make your daily dating forecast tomorrow's reality.**

This is going to make you feel fabulous! Hearing all that flattery and admiration is comforting soup for the online dater's soul. Your friends will think it's a lot of fun, too, so don't be shy when asking for their input.

CHOOSE YOUR USERNAME AND HEADLINE

Spend no more than fifteen minutes coming up with your username and headline, following the guidelines in Step 4 (see page 116).

Now, create your profile. (If you already have one, revise, update, or tweak it.) Review the guidelines in Step 4 (see page 120) before you start. Write no more than 200 words. Remember, your profile is your personal brand, and you're pitching it to all those eligible singles who just might be lucky enough to go on date number one with you. Ask a friend—a guy friend, if you're a straight woman—for his or her take on your profile. (Fresh eyes are priceless!) Adjust if necessary.

CELEBRATE YOUR ACCOMPLISHMENT!

You did it! Clap your hands, congratulate yourself, and feel amazingly proud that you have taken a huge step toward accomplishing your goal.

Days 4 and 5

- ✔ Purchase a notebook.
- ✔ Research online dating sites.
- ✔ Visit four mainstream online dating sites.
- ✔ Browse through profiles for two hours.
- ✔ Compare costs and membership options.
- ✔ Select and join one mainstream site.

RESEARCH ONLINE DATING SITES

Time for a little research! Just type "top mainstream online dating sites" or "best online dating sites" into your favorite search engine and see what comes up. Some of the women I interviewed used mainstream sites such as:

www.match.com

www.plentyoffish.com

www.okcupid.com

www.zoosk.com

www.eharmony.com

It's okay to ask for input from your single or married friends who have used dating sites.

> Tackling the tough stuff first is the best antidote to procrastination.

GO SITE SURFING

Visit the sites that pop up on your search and take notes about each one. You don't have to scrutinize every page, or write thousands of words in your notebook—just jot down what you like and don't like about each site. If cost is a factor, make sure you know which sites are free and which charge for usage.

To make your search fun and exciting, imagine that you are doing this for a friend who's just like you. Of course, you're convinced that any worthwhile person would be absolutely ecstatic at the chance to go on a date with your friend (that is, you!). So you're excited to choose the sites on which your friend would have the best chances of meeting someone great. Thinking of your search like this helps take self-doubt and negative emotions out of the equation.

But please don't obsess and drive yourself crazy trying to pick the "perfect" online dating site. At the end of the day, the perfect site will be the site that you join. Remind yourself of your ultimate goal, and know that you can always join other sites later.

BROWSE THROUGH PROFILES

Search through the profiles on each website with an age span in mind: This is a great way to get an idea of who the people on each site are—and to see what they have to say about themselves and what their photos are like. (This will give you inspiration for your profile and photos.) After you finish browsing, select three to five photos to post on your profile.

JOIN A SITE

Take all of the information you've learned about online dating and join one mainstream site to start.

Day 6

✔ Do research on four niche dating sites.

✔ Visit those sites.

✔ Browse through profiles.

✔ Compare costs and membership options.

✔ Select and join one niche site.

> There's no better place to make lots of introductions than on a dating site.

DO RESEARCH

In the same way you did with mainstream online dating sites, do an Internet search on the following terms: "niche online dating sites" or "specialty online dating sites." See what pops up: This is a great way to figure out which specialty sites are a good fit for you. I highly recommend joining both a niche site and a mainstream site. Although niche sites have far fewer members, your common interests, religion, location, or passions offer new and different opportunities.

Here are some examples of niche sites:

- **www.farmersonly.com:** A site for those who live in rural areas and don't mind getting their hands dirty. Their slogan is, "City folk just don't get it."

- **www.stitch.net:** This site is for people older than fifty looking for love, friendship, group activities, or travel. The primary markets are the United States, Australia, and Canada.

- **www.luvbyrd.com:** A site for outdoor enthusiasts. You can search for your match based on the outdoorsy stuff you love such as white water rafting, skiing, camping, ice fishing, birding, and kayaking. The site is Colorado-based, but will soon be national.

It's also a good idea to do an Internet search on a word that describes you—such as your religion, race, occupation, age, hobbies, interests, or location—in conjunction with "online dating." For instance, you might type in, "vegetarian online dating." You'll be amazed at the variety of sites your search returns! Here are a few suggestions to get you started. Have fun with it!

- African-American
- Amish
- Boating
- Books
- Canada
- Cats
- Christian
- Clowns
- Colorado
- Disabilities
- Equestrians
- Farmers
- Food allergies
- Jewish
- Mickey Mouse
- New Zealand
- Outdoors
- Over fifty
- Over forty
- Single parents
- Sports
- Star Trek
- Tattoos
- United Kingdom
- Vegetarian

Having something in common helps make an instant connection.

VISIT FOUR SITES FROM YOUR SEARCH

Just like you did with mainstream dating sites, spend a few minutes on each site, getting a sense of what each is about. Jot some notes on what you like (or dislike) about each. Compare and contrast the sites.

BROWSE THROUGH PROFILES ON THE SITES

Take a look at the profiles of people you might be interested in meeting. (It's a good idea to filter for location and age range.) Niche sites do not have as large a database as mainstream sites. If location and age are crucial for you, check these things out before you sign up.

PICK A SITE

Now it's time to select a site and join it. Think of your membership as a short-term lease on the site—just like leasing a car. As soon as your "lease" is up, you can turn in your membership and sign up for another site.

Now you've joined two online dating sites! Are you as excited as I am?

Day 7

✔ Use this as a catch-up day, if necessary.

✔ Move ahead, if you choose to.

✔ Take a day off–you deserve it!

✔ Select your personal dating trainer.

✔ Reflect on your accomplishments.

✔ Congratulate yourself for completing Week 1.

YOUR PERSONAL DATING TRAINER

The 60-Day Dating Challenge is all about you being a winner. So, think about someone in your life whose greatest pleasure would be to see you happy and in a relationship with a partner whom you love with your heart and soul. I want you to ask that person to be your personal dating trainer. Here's the best way to do it: Send your potential "trainer" an email that sounds something like the example below. (Or, if email isn't your style, meet for coffee or talk on the phone.)

Dear_____,

You have always been in my corner and have always supported me. For that I am truly grateful.

I am ready to get back out there and—yes!—date again! I can hardly believe it myself. But it's time for me to get moving— and that's where you come in.

I am taking part in a 60-Day Dating Challenge to meet new people. Some of the challenges include joining an online dating site, going to meetup groups, and going out on at least eight first dates.

I would love, love, LOVE for you to be my "super ego," my coach, and my inspiration throughout this process. Could I call you weekly to keep you apprised of how I am doing? Most of all, I just need your support to keep me motivated and driven.

Let me know what you think.

Many thanks,

_____ (Your Name)

Week 1 Planner

DAY 1	· Mark your calendar. · Check off your goals. · List your top two goals.	· List your top five deal breakers. · List your top five must-haves.
DAYS 2 & 3	· Read a friend's dating profile. · Ask two friends to text you five words that best describe you. · Ask two friends to share a funny memory of you. · Ask two friends to send you their favorite photos of you.	· Choose a username. · Select a headline. · Create your profile: "About Me" and what you are looking for. · Celebrate your accomplishment!
DAYS 4 & 5	· Purchase a notebook. · Research online dating sites. · Visit four mainstream online dating sites.	· Browse through profiles for two hours. · Compare costs and membership options. · Select and join one mainstream site
DAY 6	· Do research on four niche online dating sites. · Visit those sites. · Browse through profiles.	· Compare costs and membership options. · Select and join one niche site.
DAY 7	· Use it as a catch-up day, if necessary. · Move ahead, if you choose to. · Take a day off—you deserve it! · Select your personal dating trainer.	· Reflect on your accomplishments. · Congratulate yourself for completing Week 1.

Week 2

WEEK #2 IS ABOUT:

- Emailing your matches
- Joining a mobile app and swiping right
- Getting used to attending events and activities
- Emailing your matchmaker contacts
- Smiling and making eye contact
- Talking to a stranger

THIS WEEK YOU WILL:

- ✔ Attend a speed-dating event
- ✔ Attend a non-singles' event
- ✔ Check in with your personal dating trainer

Day 8

- ✔ Spend one hour browsing the online dating sites you selected during Week #1.
- ✔ Email three people on your mainstream site.
- ✔ Email one person on your niche site.
- ✔ Check out and join one mobile dating app.
- ✔ Send an email to five or more people who might be good matchmakers for you.
- ✔ Smile at and make eye contact with five strangers.
- ✔ Start a conversation with a stranger.

This is your first day of "date-working" (think networking—with dating as the goal). This is going to be a very productive day, because you are taking full charge of your dating life. But you're not alone. I am standing right next to you—especially when the going gets tough—and I'm cheering you on. I can't wait to celebrate your triumphs with you, and see that beautiful smile on your face.

BROWSE AND EMAIL

The fun begins now! Browse your niche site. Within twenty minutes, select one profile you like, and respond to it. Within the next twenty minutes, select three profiles on your mainstream site and send each an email. (Need a refresher course on writing a fun, intriguing first email? Review the guidelines in Step 4 on page 124.)

JOIN A MOBILE DATING APP

These apps are fun and easy to use, and aim to make meeting people simple and user-friendly. Here are a few examples:

Tinder: You can post a 500-character bio and up to six images.

Hinge: Connects you through your Facebook friends.

Coffee Meets Bagel: Sends you only one match per day.

Bumble: Ladies have to make the first move.

As with online dating sites, when it comes to mobile apps, go with your gut and join one that feels right to you.

RECRUIT YOUR MATCHMAKERS

Think of five people in your life whom you trust. They could be your sister, brother, college roommate, friend from work, or yoga buddy. Then send each an email asking them to be your "matchmaker." Knowing you as they do, these five people will keep their eyes open for potential dates for you. (Don't be shy: Your friends will be delighted that you asked!) See the sample email to the right.

A CRASH COURSE IN BEING APPROACHABLE

Think of being approachable as having your green light on—when you're approachable, it's more likely that you will be approached. Make sense? Great! Today, be extra aware of the people around you; smile at and make eye contact with five people. This is a lot easier than it sounds at first. For instance, you can smile at the clerk in the store; the woman in front of you at the post office; or the man who's standing next to you in line to order coffee. Before you know it, having your "green light" turned on will be second nature. Don't forget to start a conversation with a stranger during one of these encounters. You'll brighten someone else's day in the process.

To my favorite matchmakers:

You are at the top of my list of people I value and trust. (Don't worry: I'm not about to ask you for money!)

I signed up for a 60-Day Dating Challenge. As you might know, I am back in the world of dating, and I'd really welcome your help.

One of my assignments is to email people who are close to me, asking them to set me up with potential dates. There's no pressure: It's all about enjoying first dates and getting back in the swing of dating in general. If you have someone in mind, please let me know. I'd love it if you'd give him [or her] my phone number, and vice versa. Even if you're not sure we'd be a perfect fit, I'm open to going on a date with whomever you suggest.

Thanks in advance for helping me complete my 60-Day Dating Challenge!

With appreciation,

_____ (Your Name)

(P.S.: If I end up running away to Las Vegas with Mr. Wonderful, you'll be the first to know!)

Day 9

- ✔ Spend one hour browsing profiles online.
- ✔ Email three people on your mainstream site.
- ✔ Email two people on your niche site.
- ✔ Swipe right on seven potential matches on your mobile dating app.
- ✔ Smile at and make eye contact with five strangers.
- ✔ Start a conversation with a stranger.

BROWSE AND SEND EMAILS

Keep up the good work you started last week! This week, you'll do the same thing—but this time, email someone to whom you wouldn't ordinarily respond but whose profile gives you a good feeling. For example, maybe her profile looks interesting—but she has a motorcycle (or dog or cat or loves to go camping), and that isn't your favorite thing in the world. Instead of passing her by, take a risk and drop her a line. You might be pleasantly surprised!

SWIPE AWAY

Today is the first day using your mobile app. Don't be shy! Have fun and enjoy it. Swipe right on at least seven potential matches. (Remember, you'll only get positive feedback here; you'll only know you like each other if you both swipe right. That means you have nothing to lose!)

PRACTICE BEING APPROACHABLE

You've been doing a great job with this so far! So this week it'll be even easier to smile at and make eye contact with another five strangers. Strike up a conversation with one of them: Stand up tall and say "Hi" with energy and confidence, and see where your chat takes you.

> When you take part in activities you love, meeting people comes naturally.

Day 10

- ✔ Spend one hour browsing profiles online.
- ✔ Email four people on your main site.
- ✔ Email two people on your niche site.
- ✔ Swipe right on eight matches on your mobile dating app.
- ✔ Make eye contact with and smile at five people.

KEEP THE MOMENTUM GOING

You know what to do! Keep browsing and sending emails to people whose profiles interest you. And continue to smile at, make eye contact with, and chat with strangers you meet in your day-to-day life. You're officially becoming one of the friendliest people in town!

Also, if you haven't attended your speed-dating or non-singles' event, please schedule it now.

> **Flirting turns an ordinary conversation into an extraordinary opportunity.**

Day 11

- ✔ Check out meetup groups for single people.
- ✔ Spend one hour browsing profiles online.
- ✔ Email five people on your mainstream site.
- ✔ Email one person on your niche site.
- ✔ Swipe right on seven potential matches on your mobile dating app.
- ✔ Smile at and make eye contact with three people.
- ✔ Start a conversation with one stranger.

Day 12

- ✔ Check out meetup groups based on one of your interests.
- ✔ Swipe right on seven potential matches on your mobile app.
- ✔ Spend one hour browsing profiles online.
- ✔ Email three people on your mainstream site.
- ✔ Email one person on your niche site.
- ✔ Make eye contact with and smile at five people.

Day 13

- ✔ Post on social media that you're taking a 60-Day Dating Challenge and would welcome introductions.
- ✔ Start a conversation with a stranger.
- ✔ Spend one hour browsing profiles on your niche site.
- ✔ Email five people on your online dating sites.
- ✔ Swipe right on six people on your mobile dating app.

GO PUBLIC ON SOCIAL MEDIA ABOUT YOUR 60-DAY DATING CHALLENGE

Facebook is our go-to site when it comes to posting things we have for sale, like an exercise bike or concert tickets; for sharing the most delicious recipes; and, of course, for our photos of—well, just about everything! So why not post a "Dates Wanted" status update on Facebook (or the social media outlet of your choice)? You have nothing to lose and everything to gain.

Check out the example below. (Trust me: a post along these lines will rack up a lot

> **Never pass up an opportunity to exchange contact info. It could be your only chance to connect.**

of likes!) Plus, it'll encourage others to cheer you on, or may even inspire them to take the challenge themselves! And it'll help you stay committed. Feel free to tweak the text to match your individual voice.

GOOD HABITS

By this point, browsing profiles online and sending emails to anyone who looks interesting has become second nature. Have you gotten any replies? What about your mobile app? Have you gotten any matches? In real life, you're an old pro at meeting people by now: I bet smiling at and talking to new people is getting easier each day.

> I've signed up for a 60-Day Dating Challenge. One of my assignments is to post on social media that I'm back on the dating market. I would it love if you'd think of me if you know or meet someone who might be a great date for me. (Don't worry if you're not sure whether we'd hit it off: I'm open to it!) I've agreed to go on eight first dates and hope you can help me reach my goal. (BTW: I'm offering dinner at a five-star restaurant, complete with a limo and a night on the town, if your introduction leads me to the love of my life.) Hoping you win the prize! XOXO

Day 14

- ✔ Let one person you meet or talk to know you are on the dating market.
- ✔ Spend one hour browsing profiles online.
- ✔ Email five people on your mainstream site.
- ✔ Email one person on your niche site.
- ✔ Swipe right on five potential matches on your mobile dating app.
- ✔ Start a conversation with a stranger.
- ✔ Check in with your personal dating trainer.
- ✔ Congratulate yourself for completing Week 2!

> You never know who might know the perfect match for you.

SPREADING THE NEWS

Get into the habit of letting people you meet know you are back in the world of dating. Be sure to give them your business card so they can pass it along to any potential matches. (Better yet give them two cards—just in case!) Plus, you'll feel more and more confident every time you hear yourself tell someone you're dating again: Saying it aloud will help it feel real.

CHECK IN

In addition to sending emails, swiping, and smiling at strangers, also let your personal dating trainer know how you're doing. Share your hopes—and fears. How are you feeling? What are you most excited about?

CONGRATULATE YOURSELF!

Wow! You've completed two weeks of your 60-Day Dating Challenge. Use today to review what you've accomplished—and to think about what you need to do to move forward with courage and confidence.

Week 2 Planner

DAY 8	· Spend one hour browsing the online dating sites you selected during Week 1. · Email three people on your mainstream site. · Email one person on your niche site. · Check out and join one mobile dating app.	· Send an email to five or more people who might be good matchmakers for you. · Smile at and make eye contact with five strangers. · Start a conversation with a perfect stranger.
DAY 9	· Spend one hour browsing profiles online. · Email three people on your mainstream site. · Email two people on your niche site.	· Swipe right on seven potential matches on your mobile dating app. · Smile at and make eye contact with five strangers. · Start a conversation with a stranger.
DAY 10	· Spend one hour browsing profiles online. · Email four people on your main site. · Email two people on your niche site.	· Swipe right on eight matches on your mobile dating app. · Make eye contact with and smile at five people.
DAY 11	· Check out meetup groups for single people. · Spend one hour browsing profiles online. · Email five people on your mainstream site. · Email one person on your niche site.	· Swipe right on seven potential matches on your mobile dating app. · Smile at and make eye contact with three people. · Start a conversation with one stranger.

Week 2 Planner Continued on Next Page

Week 2 Planner (continued)

DAY 12	· Check out meetup groups based on one of your interests. · Swipe right on seven potential matches on your mobile app. · Spend one hour browsing profiles online. · Email three people on your mainstream site. · Email one person on your niche site. · Make eye contact with and smile at five people.
DAY 13	· Post on social media that you're taking a 60-Day Dating Challenge and would welcome introductions. · Start a conversation with a stranger. · Spend one hour browsing profiles on your niche site. · Email five people on your online dating sites. · Swipe right on six people on your mobile dating app.
DAY 14	· Let one person you meet or talk to know you are on the dating market. · Spend one hour browsing profiles online. · Email five people on your mainstream site. · Email one person on your niche site. · Swipe right on five potential matches on your mobile dating app. · Start a conversation with a stranger. · Check in with your personal dating trainer. · Congratulate yourself for completing Week 2!

Have you gotten used to the weekly planner? From here on, I will skip the small talk and get straight to your daily dating tasks.

Week 3

WEEK #3 IS ABOUT:

- Making eye contact with strangers
- Spreading the news that you are in the dating market
- Getting ready for your first date
- Going to a singles' event
- Winking and flirting online

THIS WEEK YOU WILL:

- Go on date number one
- Attend a singles' event with a friend
- Check in with your personal dating trainer

Week 3 Planner

DAY 15	· Use today to catch up or move ahead. · Ask for help from a friend if needed. · List what you still need to accomplish. · Smile at and make eye contact with six people. · Wink at, flirt with, like, or give a thumbs-up to five people on your online dating sites.	· Let one person you meet know you are on the dating market. · Swipe right on your mobile dating app if you have a free moment. · Email potential matches. · Take a moment to relish everything you've done so far!
DAYS 16–18	· Email five people on your mainstream site. · Email five people on your niche site. · Swipe right on nine people on your dating mobile app.	· Smile at and make eye contact with three strangers. · Start conversations with two strangers. · Let one person you meet know you are on the dating market.
DAYS 19–21	· Email five people on your mainstream dating site. · Email five people on your niche dating site. · Swipe right on nine people on your mobile dating app.	· Make small talk with three strangers. · Go on date number one. · Attend a singles' event · Congratulate yourself for completing Week 3!

Week 4

WEEK #4 IS ABOUT:

- Making small talk with strangers
- Smiling and making eye contact
- Emailing people you want to meet
- Swiping right on people you want to meet
- Checking in with your personal dating trainer
- Organizing a matchmaking party
- Winking and flirting online

THIS WEEK YOU WILL:

- Go on date number two
- Attend a singles' event with a friend
- Organize a matchmaking party
- Check in with your personal dating trainer

MS. OR MR. CONGENIALITY

Keep smiling, making eye contact, and chatting with strangers; you're practically an expert now! And, as usual, you'll email and swipe right on people on the sites and apps you've subscribed to.

HOST A MATCHMAKING PARTY

Rally a group of five or more single gals and plan a place to meet. Everyone should bring a short bio with contact info and (optional) photo of at least two single guys she knows. (Tell your girlfriends to make sure they get the okay from the guys beforehand.)

Once everyone has arrived, each gal should think about who might be a good match and why. For instance, spend a few minutes telling Amy why you think Peter would be a great date for her. If she agrees, share his contact info with her and give hers to Peter. The goal is that everyone–including you, of course!–leaves with at least one person's contact info. It's a fun way to increase your social contacts–and it's a great reason to meet up with friends.

Week 4 Planner

DAYS 22–28

- Make small talk with fourteen strangers.
- Smile at and make eye contact with twenty-one strangers.
- Wink at, flirt with, like, or give a thumbs-up to ten people who catch your eye on your online dating sites.
- Email thirty people on your mainstream dating site.
- Email fifteen people on your niche dating site.
- Swipe right on twenty people you want to meet on your mobile dating app.
- Check in with your personal dating trainer.
- Host a matchmaking party.
- Congratulate yourself for completing Week 4!

Week 5

WEEK #5 IS ABOUT

- Making small talk with strangers
- Smiling at and making eye contact with strangers
- Emailing people you want to meet
- Swiping right on people you want to meet
- Reviewing your progress
- Celebrating your success
- Checking in with your dating trainer
- Winking and flirting online

THIS WEEK YOU WILL:

- Attend one meetup group for singles
- Go on date number three
- Check in with your personal dating trainer

REFLECT ON WHERE YOU ARE

It's time to do a quick self-assessment to help you stay on track and reach your goal. The following questions will help you strategize and optimize the next four weeks. Please be brutally honest with yourself—even if it means spending more time on your 60-Day Challenge or trying something you find uncomfortable or intimidating. Remember, achieving your goals doesn't happen by accident. It happens when you're ready to do whatever's necessary to realize your dreams.

So, ask yourself the following questions, and if the answer is "no" or "not really," you need to get back on target. Don't freak out, though: Having some "nos" can actually be good. As you're halfway through your challenge, you have plenty of time to reach your goal. Think of your "nos" as extra motivation to reach your goals.

✔ Have I tried any of these bonus items?
  - Exchange phone numbers with someone I meet in person.
  - Ask someone I meet in person out on a date.
  - Journal my thoughts and feelings.

✔ Am I checking in with my personal dating trainer?

✔ Am I using the calendar to schedule dates and events?

✔ Am I on target with the number of potential dates I should contact so I can achieve my goal of eight first dates?

✔ Do I need to make more time for events or dates because I am behind schedule?

✔ Should I increase my goal of eight dates if I am almost there?

- ✔ Have I joined a mainstream site, a niche site, and a mobile dating app?
- ✔ Am I motivated to keep moving forward?
- ✔ Have I attended one speed-dating event, one non-singles' event, and one singles' event?
- ✔ Do I smile at and make eye contact with people I come in contact with?
- ✔ Have I posted my Challenge on Facebook?
- ✔ Have I started a conversation with a stranger?

Week 5 Planner

DAY 29	· Have a mini celebration because you're now halfway through your 60-Day Dating Challenge!	· Identify what you need to develop or accomplish to complete your 60-Day Dating Challenge.
DAYS 30–35	· Attend one singles' meetup group. · Go on date number three. · Make small talk with ten strangers. · Wink at, flirt with, like, or give a thumbs-up to five people who catch your eye on your online dating sites. · Smile at and make eye contact with ten strangers.	· Email twelve people you want to meet on your mainstream dating site. · Email ten people you want to meet on your niche dating site. · Swipe right on twenty people on your dating app. · Check in with your personal dating trainer. · Congratulate yourself for completing Week 5!

Week 6

WEEK #6 IS ABOUT:

- Dating
- Speed dating
- Emailing people you want to meet
- Swiping right on people you want to meet
- Chatting with strangers
- Smiling at and making eye contact with strangers
- Winking and flirting online

THIS WEEK YOU WILL:

- Go on date number four
- Attend one speed-dating event
- Check in with your personal dating trainer

Week 6 Planner

DAYS 36–42

- Go on date number four.
- Wink at, flirt with, like, or give a thumbs-up to five people who catch your eye on your online dating sites.
- Attend one speed-dating event.
- Make small talk with ten strangers.
- Smile at and make eye contact with ten strangers.
- Email twenty-one people you want to meet on your mainstream dating site.
- Email twelve people you want to meet on your niche dating site.
- Swipe right on twenty people on your mobile dating app.
- Let one person you come in contact with know you are on the dating market.
- Congratulate yourself for completing Week 6!

Week 7

WEEK #7 IS ABOUT:

- Getting ready to finish your 60-Day Dating Challenge
- Going to a meetup group
- Going on two dates
- Continuing to email people you are attracted to
- Making small talk with strangers
- Smiling at and making eye contact with strangers
- Swiping right on your mobile dating app
- Winking and flirting online

THIS WEEK YOU WILL:

- Go on date number five
- Go on date number six
- Check in with your personal dating trainer
- Attend a singles' meetup group

Week 7 Planner

DAYS 43–49

- Go on date number five.
- Go on date number six.
- Wink at, flirt with, like, or give a thumbs-up to five people who catch your eye on your online dating sites.
- Make small talk with ten strangers.
- Smile at and make eye contact with ten strangers.
- Email twenty-five people you want to meet on your mainstream dating site.
- Email twelve people you want to meet on your niche site.
- Swipe right on fifteen people on your dating app.
- Let one person you come in contact with know you are on the dating market.
- Congratulate yourself for completing Week 7!

Week 8

WEEK #8 IS ABOUT:

- Heading into the home stretch
- Feeling more courageous and confident
- Continuing to take control of your social life
- Winking and flirting online

THIS WEEK YOU WILL:

- Go on date number seven
- Go on date number eight
- Go to one social event
- Check in with your personal dating trainer

Week 8 Planner

DAYS 50–56

- Go on date number seven.
- Go on date number eight.
- Wink at, flirt with, like, or give a thumbs-up to five people who catch your eye on your online dating sites.
- Go to one social event.
- Make small talk with ten strangers.
- Smile at and make eye contact with ten strangers.
- Email ten people you want to meet on your mainstream dating site.
- Email five people you want to meet on your niche site.
- Swipe right on twenty people on your dating app.
- Congratulate yourself for completing Week 8!

Week 9

You have done it!! For the last sixty days, you have dated, swiped, emailed, chatted, smiled, and broken out of your comfort zone. You are on your way to finding the love you deserve! If you met someone who makes you smile and feel terrific in their presence, enjoy it–you deserve it!

WEEK #9 IS ABOUT:
- Reflecting on your accomplishments
- Planning for the future

THIS WEEK YOU WILL:
- Attend one non-singles' meetup group
- Check in with your personal dating trainer

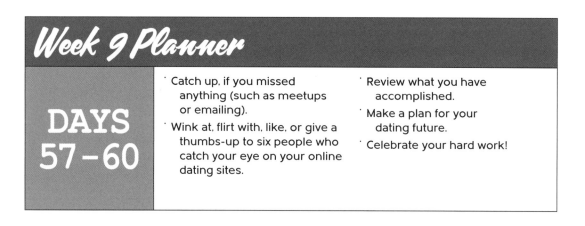

Week 9 Planner

DAYS 57–60

- Catch up, if you missed anything (such as meetups or emailing).
- Wink at, flirt with, like, or give a thumbs-up to six people who catch your eye on your online dating sites.
- Review what you have accomplished.
- Make a plan for your dating future.
- Celebrate your hard work!

Review and Reflection

Wow! You did it. Congratulations. You're at the end of your 60-Day Dating Challenge! I'm sure you found it challenging and even difficult at times, but you stayed with it. And I'm so glad you did!

Now let's talk about how things went. That's right: I want to hear the best and the worst! Since I really do want to know everything about how your challenge went, I'd love it if you'd email me at 60daydatingchallenge@gmail.com and tell me your story.

Here are some things to think about as you reflect:

THE BEST

- What did you love about the 60-Day Dating Challenge?
- How did it help you?
- What did you learn about yourself?

THE AWFUL

- What was the hardest part of the 60-Day Dating Challenge?
- What did you like least about the challenge?
- What made you want to give up?
- How did you keep yourself motivated and driven?

Thank yourself for investing your heart and soul in the 60-Day Dating Challenge. You did an amazing job!

Conclusion

Welcome to your next chapter!

You have crossed the finish line of your 60-Day Dating Challenge, and you're ready to continue on your dating journey. Thanks for your incredible resilience, your unwavering strength, and your joyful attitude along the way. I watched you (from afar) totally and diligently investing in yourself—even when you felt frustrated or overwhelmed—to create a future that's everything you want it to be.

If you met someone you adore, that's fabulous. I'm so happy for you! If you didn't, it's not a big deal. (Truly.) You've still achieved something spectacular: You now have the courage, confidence, and know-how to embrace and enjoy each date. And you have this book for future reference. Keep it in an easy-to-reach place so you can refer back to it anytime you need a pep talk or a little extra encouragement. And, the best part is, when you return to this book in the future, you'll be pleasantly surprised by how far you've come. (I'm not surprised, though: I knew you could do it!)

Since you're now a dating expert, you can pay it forward—to your friends, relatives, and work buddies who can benefit from the challenge just as you have. Share your successes with them—help them get started and assure them they can count on you to support them through their journeys. (Plus, if you're still searching for Mr. Right, supporting someone else will keep you motivated to continue on your dating expeditions.) Or, if you and a few friends are currently going through, or have recently completed, the 60-Day Dating Challenge, think about meeting up from time to time to share your experiences. It's a great way to stay motivated—and, of course, it's lots of fun!

I hope I've been a part of your healing process. And now that you've come so far, if someone close to you has been devastated by a broken heart, you'll be able to tell her: *You will be okay; you will survive, and, yes, you will be happy.* You are living proof.

Wishing you the love-filled life that you deserve!

Acknowledgments

A huge thanks to Ken Fund, COO of The Quarto Group, for believing in me and for making *Dating Again with Courage and Confidence* a reality. It would not have happened without you, and for that I am so very grateful!

My sincere gratitude goes to my incredible and talented acquiring editor Jess Haberman, who from day one was the most caring, helpful, and calming editor I could ask for. Jess, thanks for being there for me every step of the way and for your special way of always making me feel totally and completely supported. Your insight and guidance were outstanding. I could not have done it without you.

Heartfelt thanks to Megan Buckley, my developmental editor, who made sure that my every word came alive. I loved the way you were able to dot all the I's and cross all the T's. Your kindness and sensitivity were greatly appreciated.

This book is an amazing creation supported by the inspiration, dedication, wisdom, marketing, and creativity of a very gifted group of people. My heartfelt thanks and appreciation to the amazing team at Quarto: Publisher, Winnie Prentiss; Project Editor, Meredith Quinn; Art Director, David Martinell; Creative Director, Regina Grenier; Marketing Manager, Steven Pomije; and Designer/Illustrator, Mattie Wells.

Words cannot describe how incredible my husband Jim Mullin has been throughout the entire process of writing this book. Just about every hour, I would ask, "Hon, do you have a minute?" (aka could you listen to what I just wrote?) I can't thank you enough for your unwavering support, patience, encouragement, and all of your invaluable input. Most of all, thank you for the love you demonstrate to me each and every day. Without you, this book would not have been possible!

A very special thank you to Juliet, who, on a moment's notice, would come to my rescue with all of her personal experiences and wisdom about being single. You read every word of the manuscript with such interest and love. You are a dream come true.

Thank you to my wonderful friends, who always had the time to listen to parts of the manuscript and helped me get to the finish line: Marianne, Daniella, the Carols, Roz, Theresa, and Stephanie.

A loving thanks to my niece Jaime for sharing her insight on how to deal with a breakup.

Thank you to Trish McDermott, the former VP for Romance at Match.com, for convincing me that I should write a book to help women get back into the dating world.

To my wonderful family for always being so reassuring and always being proud of me, a very special thank you. I love you all.

Thank you from the bottom of my heart to all of the women I interviewed. Your courage, resilience, and honesty are reflected everywhere in this book, especially the wisdom you gave me about what helped you get through your loss.

A tremendous thank you to all of my clients and workshop participants. Each one of you has inspired me to write this book. You taught me the power of perseverance and hope.

Lastly, to my parents, Rozzie and Joey. You wiped my tears, mended my broken heart, and taught me by example how to deal with loss and to always be grateful. You gave me the greatest gift in the whole world—your love for each other. I love and miss you both so much.

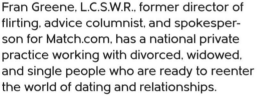

About the Author

Fran Greene, L.C.S.W.R., former director of flirting, advice columnist, and spokesperson for Match.com, has a national private practice working with divorced, widowed, and single people who are ready to reenter the world of dating and relationships.

Fran is the author of *The Flirting Bible* and is well known as The Flirting, Dating, and Relationship Coach. She is successful in helping single people navigate the complex maze of online dating. As a licensed social worker, Fran has helped hundreds of women and men find love and happiness. She also works with couples who want to transform their troubled relationships into connected, loving ones.

Fran has appeared on the *Today Show*, *Dateline NBC*, and *Good Day New York* and has been featured in the *Chicago Tribune*, the *New York Times*, *BravoTV.com*, *Cosmopolitan*, and *Seventeen*. Fran is known for her insight, humor, and compassion. She provides powerful, practical tips and realistic ways to date again at any age.

She lives in New York with her husband. To learn more about Fran, visit her at www.frangreene.com.

Index